Be Who
You Are

English edition published by Scepter Publishers, Inc., copyright © 2018
info@scepterpublishers.org
www.scepterpublishers.org
800-322-8773
New York

Cover design by Alston Taggart
Text design by Rose Design

Library of Congress Cataloging-in-Publication Data available.

ISBN: 978-1-59417-322-6

Printed in the United States of America

Be Who
You Are

Scepter

Contents

Authors

Alfonso Aguiló: has been principal of Tajamar School in Madrid; he is president of the Spanish Confederation of Centers of Education. He has published eleven books on topics of education and anthropology, translated into several languages.

Carlos Ayxelà: is a priest, with degrees in humanities and journalism and a doctorate in philosophy from the University of Montreal. He is currently carrying out research at the Pontifical University of the Holy Cross in Rome on the theology of Joseph Ratzinger in light of St. Augustine's concept of memory.

José María Barrio Maestre: has a doctorate in philosophy and teaches at the Complutense University in Madrid.

José Benito Cabaniña Magide: has degrees in journalism and theology from the University of Navarra. He has been chaplain of several university residences in Pamplona, Madrid, and Valladolid.

Javier Cabanyes Truffino: has a doctorate in medicine (neurology) and is professor of psychopathology at the Complutense University in Madrid.

Juan Ramón García-Morato Soto: is a doctor and priest, with a doctorate in theology. He is a professor of anthropology at the University of Navarra, and has been a chaplain at this university since 1985.

Javier Láinez: is rector of the Basilica of St. Michael in Madrid. He has degrees in law and philosophy. He has worked for over twenty years in various schools.

Javier Sesé: is a priest, with degrees in mathematics and theology. Since 1985 he has been professor of spiritual theology at the University of Navarra.

Rodolfo Valdés: is a priest, and has a doctorate in philosophy. He is carrying out research in the area of ethics and forming the person.

Wenceslao Vial: is professor of psychology and spiritual life in the faculty of theology at the Pontifical University of the Holy Cross in Rome; a priest and doctor, he has a doctorate in philosophy.

Foreword

History recounts that in the times of ancient Rome pirates gradually took control of the Mediterranean Sea. Pompey the Great, consul of Rome, acted vigorously to end this scourge, but he also tried to treat the pirates in a humane way. The outlaws, surprised by the leniency shown them, praised the Consul: "The more you act like a man, the more you resemble the gods."

These words from the distant past can help us reflect on our own life. The first requirement for an upright character is acting as a human being. It is only on this foundation that a mature personality can be forged—a strong and friendly way of being that becomes the support for a rich spiritual life redounding to the benefit of many other people.

This book arose from an interdisciplinary group that gathered together ideas on how to develop a healthy, well-rounded personality.[1] The fact that the

---

1. These contributions first appeared on *www.opusdei.org*, and are now presented here in a fuller form.

contributors come from a wide variety of backgrounds and interests, has greatly helped to enrich the book's content. As theologians, philosophers, priests, doctors, educators, and psychologists, they have all made contributions based on their own experience and expertise.

The book focuses on the features proper to a mature personality, with special attention to a Christian's spiritual life. The Catholic Church has a long tradition of teachers of the spiritual life who provide a coherent synthesis of the various factors that converge to form a healthy personality. Among these, St. Josemaría Escrivá has been a key source of inspiration. The teachings of this saint contain valuable advice on the importance of strengthening human virtues as the foundation for the supernatural virtues, on the need to form Christians with their own criteria and standards, and on the essential requirement for "unity of life" in each person.

Although the book discusses a wide variety of circumstances, its focus above all is on those going through crucial phases in personality development, especially between the ages of fifteen and thirty (adolescents and young adults), and on those who in one way or another are involved in their formation.

In the universe, we can behold a harmony provided by fixed laws, the orderly development of seeds that become fruit-yielding trees, and the steady movement of the stars. And we can also see how remarkably alike are human activities and endeavors across distinct races and cultures. Not surprisingly, then, when seeking the signs of a maturing personality, we find that they fall into a coherent order, a process with clear steps.

The book's first chapter, which serves as an introduction, explains what is meant by maturity and temperament. It highlights some positive features of the process of growth, with special reference to Christ as our model and the transforming force of grace over time. As Pope Francis wrote, "Were maturity merely the development of something already present in our genetic code, not much would have to be done. But prudence, good judgement and common sense are dependent not on purely quantitative growth factors, but rather on a whole series of things that come together deep within each person, or better, at the very core of our freedom."[2]

The chapters that follow consider other signs of maturity, each of which, in its own way, can help a person to think about their own level of maturity. One sign

---

2. Pope Francis, Apostolic Exhortation *Amoris laetitia* (March 19, 2016), 262.

is autonomy, which, combined with a healthy dependence on others, is exercised with freedom and responsibility and the awareness that we have a mission in life and that many great things depend on us. Another key sign of maturity is the healthy self-esteem that comes from knowing we are children of God, which enables us to put up with small or great setbacks in life. Maturity also requires grounding our lives on ideals and values through the exercise of the virtues, without falling into a false perfectionism. It requires a coherent and unified life, the ability to dialogue and establish cordial relationships with everyone. Maturity entails the capacity for empathy, whereby a person learns to understand others and to share in their sufferings, and is able to make the truth lovable. Finally, maturity comes to fruition in the heart of a family, where we learn a spirit of cooperation and sacrifice and the need to give ourselves to others.

The final chapter, which deals with personal identity, sums up the entire process of maturing. As we come to know who we are and the goal of our life, and as we acquire a serene conquest of our self-identity, we are led to the discovery that God's plan for each person has a supernatural horizon, which is the only one capable of quenching the human heart's hunger for happiness.

Thus we discover who we really are, in the serene struggle to love Jesus Christ and all men and women in Him. We discover the touchstone of authentic love: "Sometimes we speak of love as if it were an impulse to self-satisfaction or a mere means to selfish fulfillment of one's own personality. But that's not love. True love means going out of oneself, giving oneself."[3]

We trust that readers will find these pages useful for coming to know themselves better and finding ways to give themselves more effectively to others. I thank the authors for their important contributions—among them, Carlos Ayxelà and Rodolfo Valdés, who helped to revise the articles and give them more unity. I also extend appreciation to all those who have read the manuscript and offered their suggestions, especially Enrique Prada, for his contributions. Special gratitude is owed to Fr. Javier Yaniz for his work of inspiration and coordination of the entire project.

Wenceslao Vial

---

3. Josemaría Escrivá, *Christ Is Passing By* (New York: Scepter Publishers, 2002), no. 43.

1

A Personality Identified with Christ

Javier Sesé

A MATURE PERSON HAS A NOBLE, CLEAR
AND COHERENT LIFE-PROJECT.

Why do I react that way? Why am I like this? Can I change? These are questions we sometimes ask ourselves. And at times we pose them about others: *Why is that person like that?* Let us take a deeper look at these questions in view of our goal: to become more like Jesus Christ, allowing him to act in our lives. This process encompasses all the dimensions of someone who, in becoming divinized, retains the features of an authentic humanity while raising them in accord with our Christian vocation.

Christ is true God and true man: *perfectus Deus, perfectus homo*. In him we contemplate the truly complete human being. "Christ the Redeemer fully reveals man to himself. If we may use the expression, this is the human dimension of the mystery of the Redemption. In this dimension man finds again the greatness, dignity and value that belong to his humanity."[1]

The new life we received at Baptism is destined to be built up "until we all attain to the unity of the faith and of the knowledge of the Son of God, to mature manhood, to the measure of the stature of the fulness of Christ" (Eph 4:13). The divine element, the supernatural one, is decisive in personal holiness, and it unites and harmonizes all the human facets. But we should not forget that included here, as an intrinsic and necessary element, is the human one: "If we accept the responsibility of being children of God, we will realize that God wants us to be very human. Our heads should indeed be touching heaven, but our feet should be firmly on the ground. The price of living as Christians is not that of ceasing to be human or of abandoning the effort to acquire those virtues which some have even without

---

1. John Paul II, Encyclical *Redemptor Hominis* (March 4, 1979), 10.

knowing Christ. The price paid for each Christian is the redeeming Blood of our Lord and he, I insist, wants us to be both very human and very divine, struggling each day to imitate him who is *perfectus Deus, perfectus homo.*"[2]

THE TASK OF BUILDING CHARACTER

The action of grace in souls goes hand in hand with growth in human maturity, with perfecting our character. So while cultivating the supernatural virtues, a Christian who seeks holiness will strive to attain the ways of acting and thinking that characterize someone as being mature and balanced. He or she will be motivated not merely by the desire for perfection but by the eagerness to reflect Christ's life. Thus St. Josemaría encourages us to examine ourselves: "My son, where do men find in you the Christ they are looking for? In your pride? In your desire to impose yourself on others? In those little character defects which you don't wish to overcome? In your stubbornness? Is Christ to be found there? No, he is not!" The answer gives us the clue to this endeavor: "You need to have your own

---

2. Josemaría Escrivá, *Friends of God* (New York: Scepter, 1997), no. 75.

personality, agreed. But you should try to make it conform exactly to Christ's."[3]

Our personality is influenced first of all by what we have inherited, which began to be manifested from birth, often called temperament. It is also influenced by factors connected with our upbringing, personal decisions, relationships with others and with God, and many other factors, perhaps even unconscious ones. All this leads to a variety of types of personalities or temperaments (extroverted or timid, spirited or reserved, carefree or apprehensive, etc.), expressed in one's way of working, of interacting with others, of considering daily events. These elements influence each person's moral life, by facilitating the development of certain virtues or, if the effort to attain these is lacking, the appearance of defects. For example, an enterprising personality can make it easier to acquire the virtue of industriousness, provided one has the discipline needed to avoid the defects of inconstancy and activism.

God counts on our personality in leading us along the path to holiness. Each person's way of being is like fertile land that needs to be cultivated. If we

---

3. Josemaría Escrivá, *The Forge* (New York: Scepter, 1992), no. 468.

patiently and cheerfully remove the stones and weeds that impede the action of grace, it will begin to "bring forth grain, some a hundredfold, some sixty, some thirty" (Mt 13:8). All men and women can make fruitful the talents received from God's hands, provided they allow themselves to be transformed by the action of the Holy Spirit, forging a personality that reflects Christ's face. But this does not imply losing one's own personal traits. St. Josemaría insisted: "you have to be different from one another, as the saints in heaven are different, each having their own personal and special characteristics."[4]

While we need to strengthen and polish our own personality in keeping with a Christian way of living, we aren't striving to become some kind of "superman." Rather the model is always Jesus Christ, who has a human nature like ours, but perfect in its normality and elevated by grace. Certainly, we also have a lofty example in Our Lady: in Mary we see the fullness of humanity—and of normality. The proverbial humility and simplicity of Mary, probably the most cherished of her qualities in the entire Christian tradition, along

---

4. Josemaría Escrivá, *The Way* (New York: Scepter, 1992), no. 947.

with her closeness and tender affection for all her children, the virtues of a good mother, are the best confirmation of her perfection. Although Mary is still a creature we can tell her: "greater than you, none but God!"[5] For she is so fully human, so charmingly feminine: the Lady *par excellence*!

HUMAN AND
SUPERNATURAL MATURITY

The word "maturity" means being ripe, fully developed, and by extension it refers to the fullness of being. Therefore, its best paradigm can be found in our Lord's life. Contemplating in the Gospels shows how Christ dealt with people, his fortitude in suffering, and his decisiveness in undertaking the mission received from his Father. Here we have the criterion of maturity.

At the same time, our faith incorporates all the noble values found in different cultures. It also purifies the traditional criteria of human maturity. This has been done throughout the history of Christian spirituality. For example, the Greco-Roman classical world, which the Fathers of the Church so wisely

---

5. Escrivá, *The Way*, no. 496.

Christianized, especially placed wisdom and prudence at the center of the ideal of human maturity, understood with various nuances. The Christian philosophers and theologians of the early Church enriched this view, pointing out the pre-eminence of the theological virtues, especially charity, which as St. Paul said, "binds everything together in perfect harmony" (Col 3:14), and gives form to all the virtues.

In our day and age the study of human maturity has been complemented by the different perspectives offered by the modern sciences. These findings are useful to the extent that they start from a vision of the human person open to the Christian message. Thus, some tend to distinguish three key fields of maturity: intellectual, emotional and social. Significant features of intellectual maturity include: an adequate self-concept (with a close correspondence between how one views oneself and how one really is, firmly based on sincerity with oneself); clearly defined personal goals and purposes, with open and unlimited horizons; a harmonious set of values; ethical and moral certainty; a healthy realism in relation to oneself and others; the capacity for reflection and calm analysis of problems; creativity and initiative; and so on.

Some features of emotional maturity, without trying to be exhaustive, would include: balanced reactions to life's events, without being discouraged by failure or emboldened by success; the capacity for flexible and constructive self-control; the ability to love and to give oneself generously to others; confidence and firmness in decisions and commitments; serenity and constancy in facing challenges and difficulties; optimism, cheerfulness, friendliness and good humor.

Finally, as elements of social maturity we find: a sincere affection for others, respecting their rights and seeking to discover and remedy their needs; being understanding when faced with a diversity of opinions, values or cultural features, without falling into prejudices; independence and a critical capacity in the face of a dominant culture, pressure groups or fashions; naturalness in one's behavior that leads to acting without mere conventionalism; the capacity to listen and understand; the ability to work with others.

A PATH TO MATURITY

We could summarize these traits by saying that the mature person develops a noble, clear and coherent life-project, with the positive outlook needed to carry it out readily. In any case maturity requires time, and passes through various moments and stages. Its growth is usually gradual, although specific events in a person's life can lead to rapid advances. For example, the birth of a first child is a milestone that can suddenly wake a person up to the implications of this new responsibility. Or going through serious economic hardships can result in a new evaluation of what is truly important in life, etc.

The transforming power of grace is a significant factor in the path to maturity. We see in the better-known saints their high ideals, their firm convictions, their humility (the most adequate self-concept), their boundless creativity and initiative, their capacity for self-giving and love shown in deeds, their infectious optimism, their effective and universal openness, expressed in their apostolic zeal. A clear example is the life of St. Josemaría, who from his youth felt the action of grace in strengthening his personality. Despite confronting many difficulties, when still quite young he felt within himself a peace of mind out of the ordinary: "I believe that the Lord has put in my soul another characteristic: peace—the ability to have peace and to give peace—judging by what I see in the people I deal with or whom I direct."[6] The words from the psalm could quite appropriately be applied to him: *Super senes intellexi quia mandata tua quaesivi* (Ps 118, Vulgate): I have more understanding than the elders, because I keep your commands. But all of this is compatible with the reality that maturity is usually acquired over time, through confronting the failures and successes that are part of the working of Divine Providence.

RELYING ON GRACE AND TIME

Although it is often clear when a person has reached a certain stage of maturity in life, the task of bettering oneself is a lifetime project. Self-knowledge and self-acceptance will give us the peace needed so as not to become discouraged. This does not mean being content with what we have already achieved. Rather it means recognizing that the heroism of holiness does not require perfection or aspiring to an idealized way of being. Holiness requires a patient day-by-day struggle, recognizing our mistakes and asking for forgiveness.

---

6. Josemaría Escrivá, *Intimate Notes*, no. 1095, quoted in Andrés Vázquez de Prada, *The Founder of Opus Dei*, vol. I (New York: Scepter, 2001), p. 481.

"The true-to-life stories of Christian heroes resemble our own experience: they fought and won; they fought and lost. And then, repentant, they returned to the fray."[7] God counts on our effort over time to polish our way of being. As someone told a woman with a strong temperament towards the end of her life: "'Dora, nobody who saw you then would believe it if they could see you now! You're like a different person.' She laughed, knowing very well what I meant."[8] This person helped Dora realize how, over the years, with patient effort and God's grace, her character had reached a degree of equanimity that moderated her strong reactions. The woman referred to here is Dora del Hoyo, who after many years spent putting care and love into household tasks, died with a reputation for holiness the day before she turned 90, happy and still young at heart.

In this endeavor we can always count on our Lord's help and Mary's motherly care: "Our Lady does just that with us. She helps us to grow as human

---

7. Escrivá, *Christ Is Passing By*, no. 76.

8. Recollections of Rosalia Lopez Martinez, Rome, November 29, 2006 (AGP, DHA, T-1058), as quoted in Javier Medina, *Dora del Hoyo: A Lighted Lamp* (New York: Scepter, 2014), p. 94.

beings and in the faith, to be strong and never to fall into the temptation of being human beings and Christians in a superficial way, but to live responsibly, to strive ever higher."[9]

In subsequent chapters, we will consider various aspects of character development and point out some key features of Christian maturity. We will contemplate the edifice that the Holy Spirit seeks to raise up in our soul with our active collaboration. And we will look at the characteristics that the foundations should have to ensure that the structure is firm, and how to remedy any cracks that might appear.

---

9. Pope Francis, Address before Recital of the Holy Rosary (May 4, 2013).

2

Authors of Our Own Lives

Juan Ramón García-Morato

<small>OPTING FOR GOD MEANS ACCEPTING HIS INVITATION
TO WRITE OUR OWN BIOGRAPHY WITH HIS HELP.</small>

"I ask you to be builders of the future, to work for a better world. Dear young people, please, don't be observers of life, but get involved. Jesus did not remain an observer, but he immersed himself. Don't be observers, but immerse yourself in the reality of life, as Jesus did."[1] These words of Pope Francis to young people immediately raise some questions that the Roman Pontiff

---

1. Francis, Prayer Vigil with the Young People during the Apostolic Journey to Rio de Janeiro for World Youth Day (July 27, 2013).

13

himself formulated: "[s]hall we begin? Where? With you and me! Each one of you, once again in silence, ask yourself: if I must begin with myself, where exactly do I start? Each one of you, open his or her heart, so that Jesus may tell you where to start."[2] To be protagonists in world events, we first need to be protagonists in our own lives. We need to acquire self-mastery.

FREE AND CONDITIONED

Taking control of our own lives requires recognizing that while family or social circumstances influence our character, they do not determine it absolutely. The same is true of the most basic instincts that come from heredity and bodily constitution. These instinctive ways of acting can be molded and guided by the exercise of a will that heeds the dictates of a well-formed reason.

Our personality is forged to the extent that we make free decisions, since our actions not only alter our environments but also shape who we are. Although at times we aren't fully aware of it, the repetition of acts leads us to acquire particular customs or attitudes in facing reality. Therefore when we explain the reason for

---

2. Francis.

our spontaneous reactions, rather than saying "that's the way I am," we should often admit: "that's the way I have made myself."

Our lives are conditioned by factors that are often difficult to control: for example, the quality of family relationships, the social environment in which we grow up, an illness that limits us. Although often we are unable to ignore or undo these limitations, we can certainly change our attitudes in confronting them, especially if we are aware that nothing escapes God's provident care. "It is important to keep reminding ourselves that Jesus did not address himself to a privileged set of people; he came to reveal the universal love of God to us. God loves all mankind, and he wants all to love him."[3]

In any situation, even one that entails great limitations, we can offer God and our neighbors deeds of love, no matter how small these may seem. Who knows how great is the value of a smile in the midst of suffering, offered to our Lord in union with the Cross, of patiently accepting small annoyances and setbacks! Nothing can quench a limitless love, a love stronger than suffering, loneliness, abandonment, betrayal, slander, physical and moral suffering, and even death itself.

---

3. Escrivá, *Christ Is Passing By*, no. 110.

AUTHOR OF OUR OWN LIVES

Our freedom brings with it the responsibility to discover our personal talents, virtues and skills, to be
thankful for them and draw out as much fruit as possible. But we should never forget that what most firmly
shapes a Christian personality are the gifts of God that
configure the deepest recesses of our beings. Preemi-
nent among these is the immense gift of divine filiation
received at Baptism, thanks to which the Father sees in
us the image of his Son Jesus. This likeness, although
imperfect, since we are limited creatures, becomes pro-
gressively clearer through the sacrament of Confirmation and the transforming forgiveness received in the
sacrament of Penance, and in a special way through
communion with the Body and Blood of Christ.

Starting from these gifts received from God's hand,
every person, like it or not, is the author of his or her
own life. In the words of St. John Paul II: "all men and
women are entrusted with the task of crafting their
own life. In a certain sense, they are to make of it a work
of art, a masterpiece."[4] We are the masters of our own
actions. "It was he who created man in the beginning,
and he left him in the power of his own inclination"

---

4. John Paul II, Letter to Artists (April 4, 1999), no. 2.

(Sir 15:14). It is we, if we so wish, who hold firmly to the tiller of our lives in the midst of all the storms and difficulties.

We are free! This discovery can bring with it some trepidation: *Where will my life take me?* But above all it brings joy. "God in creating us has run the risk and the adventure of our freedom. He wanted a history that would be a true one, the product of genuine decisions, and not a fiction or some sort of game."[5] In this adventure we are not alone. We count, first of all, on God's help, who offers us a mission. Next we count on the help of family members and friends, and also those who happen to be alongside us.

Being authors of our own lives is not to deny that we are dependent in many respects on others. And realizing that this dependence is reciprocal, we can also say that we are interdependent. Our freedom therefore is not self-sufficient. It would remain empty if we did not use it to commit ourselves to magnanimous, great undertakings. Our freedom is for self-giving; or in other words, the only genuine freedom is one that involves self-giving.

---

5. Josemaría Escrivá, "The Riches of the Faith," as published in *ABC*, Madrid, (November 2, 1969).

A PATH FOR EACH ONE'S LIFE

St. Josemaría used to recall a poster he saw in Burjasot (Valencia, Spain), shortly after the end of the Spanish civil war, containing advice he often quoted in his preaching: *Each wayfarer should follow his own path.* Each has to follow the path of his or her own vocation in a very personal way, with its very specific requirements. "You can travel on the right, on the left, or zig-zagging, on foot or on horseback. There are a hundred thousand ways to go along the divine path."[6] Each person is the principal actor in the history of his or her holiness. We each need to leave a distinctive mark on every facet of our own makeup and personality, striving never simply to be "carried along" by events,

"It is freely, as children and not as slaves, that we follow the path which our Lord has marked out for each one of us. We relish our freedom of action as a gift from God."[7] This freedom, a mark of human dignity, goes hand in hand with the responsibility of knowing we are God's handiwork. Each human being is a divine dream that becomes a reality when we experience God's

---

6. Josemaría Escrivá, Letter (February 2, 1945), no. 19.

7. Escrivá, *Friends of God*, no. 35.

unconditional love that seeks our response. God's love affirms our freedom and raises it to unexpected heights with his grace.

ACCOMPANIED ALONG THE PATH

Within the divine plan, life is meant to be shared with others. God counts on the mutual help that human beings give to each other. We experience this every day, for many times each day we are unable to meet our most basic and urgent needs on our own. No one can be completely autonomous. At a deeper level, each person senses the need to open up his or her life to someone else, to give and receive love. "No one lives alone. No one sins alone. No one is saved alone. The lives of others continually spill over into mine: in what I think, say, do and achieve. And conversely, my life spills over into that of others: for better and for worse."[8]

This natural openness to others reaches its maximum expression in God's redemptive plan. When we recite the Apostles' Creed, we confess that we believe in the *communion of saints*, a communion that is at the heart of the Church. Therefore, in the spiritual life it

---

8. Benedict XVI, Encyclical *Spe salvi* (November 30, 2007), no. 48.

is also essential to learn to count on the help of others who are involved in one way or another in our relationship with God. We receive the faith through the teaching of our parents and catechists. We take part in the sacraments celebrated by a minister of the Church. We seek the spiritual advice of another brother or sister in the faith, who also prays for us; and so on.

Knowing that we are accompanied in the Christian life fills us with joy and peace, without diminishing our own effort to achieve holiness. Although we often let ourselves be led by the hand, our role is not limited to only that. St. Josemaría, referring to the spiritual life, said that "Advice, however, does not eliminate personal responsibility."[9] And he concluded by stressing that spiritual guidance should aim to develop men and women with their own Christian standards.[10] Therefore, we don't want others to make our own decisions for us, nor do we want to fail to take on with personal responsibility the tasks we have at hand.

While recognizing the indispensable help provided by others, we also need to be aware that in the spiritual life it is God who works through them to convey to us

9. Josemaría Escrivá, *Conversations with St. Josemaría* (New York: Scepter, 2007), no. 93.

10. Escrivá.

his light and strength. This gives us confidence to continue walking towards holiness when, for one reason or another, the persons who played an important role in our Christian life are absent. Thus we also enjoy a deep freedom of spirit in relation to the people God has placed at our side, whom we love through the heart of Christ, and whose help we deeply appreciate.

FREE TO LOVE UNCONDITIONALLY

Christians know that personal fulfillment comes as the result of a free and total self-giving to the love of a God who is our Creator, Redeemer, and Sanctifier. The gifts we have received reach their fruition by opening us to God's grace, as the experience of so many saints demonstrates. In allowing God to enter into their lives, the saints placed themselves lovingly at his service, as Our Lady did at the moment of the Annunciation when "she gives her firm reply: *Fiat!* Be it done unto me according to thy word! This is the fruit of the best freedom of all, the freedom of opting for God."[11]

When we opt for God, we direct our dreams and energies toward what is most worthwhile in life. We

---

11. Escrivá, *Friends of God*, no. 25.

fulfill the ultimate meaning of freedom, which is not simply to choose this or that, but to dedicate our lives to something great, accepting definitive commitments. Dedicating our talents to following Christ, which at times requires rejecting other options, is what brings real happiness, "a hundredfold" on earth and "eternal life" (Mt 19:29). It also reflects a high degree of inner maturity, because only those with deep personal convictions can commit their whole heart: "I opt for God because I want to, freely, without compulsion of any kind."[12]

ABANDONING PAST, PRESENT AND FUTURE IN GOD'S HANDS

The soul that opts for God acquires an inner peace that rises above any tribulation. "I know whom I have believed" (2 Tim 1:12). These words express St. Paul's confidence of being faithful to his vocation as an apostle to the Gentiles despite all the difficulties. Those who ground their life on God acquire an unshakeable security that allows them to give themselves to others: whether in celibacy, for apostolic reasons, or in marriage, or in so many other paths that Christian life

---

12. *Friends of God*, no. 35.

can take. It is a self-giving that spans past, present and future, as St. Josemaría prayed: "My Lord and my God: into your hands I abandon the past and the present and the future, what is small and what is great, what amounts to a little and what amounts to a lot, things temporal and things eternal."[13]

No one can change the past. But God knows the true meaning of each person's history. In the Sacrament of Reconciliation, he can forgive any sin and reintegrate these events harmoniously in the life of his children. Everything works for our good (cf. Romans 8:28), even the mistakes we may have made, if we have recourse to God's mercy and with his grace seek to live more attentive to him in the present. Thus we can look confidently towards the future, because we know we are in the hands of a Father who loves us. When we are in God's hands, we fall and always get up in God's hands!

Opting for God means accepting his invitation to write our own biographies with his help. Humbly recognizing our freedom as a gift, we will employ it to carry out, accompanied by so many other people, the mission God has entrusted to us. And we will joyfully

---

13. Escrivá, *The Way of the Cross* (New York: Scepter, 2011), VII, no. 3.

experience that his plans exceed all our expectations, as St. Josemaría once told a youngster: "Let yourself be carried by grace! Let your heart fly! Write your own little novel: a novel of sacrifice and heroism. With God's grace, your dreams will fall short."[14]

---

14. Josemaría Escrivá as quoted in notes taken at a get-together on June 29, 1974.

3

A Healthy Self-esteem

Javier Cabanyes

<small>SELF-ESTEEM FLOURISHES UNDER
THE SHELTER OF HUMILITY.</small>

"You were ransomed . . . not with perishable things such as silver or gold, but with the precious blood of Christ" (1 Pet 1:18–19). St. Peter reminds the first Christians that their very existence has acquired an immeasurable value, since they have become the object of God's overwhelming, redemptive love. Through the gift of divine filiation Christ fills with security our passage through this world. A young fellow once told St. Josemaría spontaneously: "'Father,' said that big fellow, a good student at the Central University (I wonder what has become of him), 'I

25

was thinking of what you told me—that I'm a son of God! And I found myself walking along the street, head up, chin out, and a proud feeling inside . . . a son of God!' With sure conscience I advised him to foster that 'pride.'"[1]

Recognizing Our Greatness

What does it mean "to foster that pride"? It is certainly not a matter of conjuring up imaginary virtues, nor of leading a self-sufficient existence that sooner or later betrays us. Rather it means recognizing the greatness of our creaturely condition. The human being is the "only creature on earth which God willed for itself."[2] Created in God's image and likeness, we are called to develop fully this image by an ever-closer identification with Christ through the action of grace.

Such a sublime vocation provides the foundation for a healthy self-esteem. The light of faith enables us to judge rightly our achievements and failures. The serene acceptance of our own identities shapes

---

1. Escrivá, *The Way*, no. 274.

2. Vatican Council II, Pastoral Constitution on the Church in the Modern World *Gaudium et spes*, 24.

our ways of being and acting in society. It also fosters self-confidence and lessens fear and shyness, and helps prevent us from acting rashly; it makes it easier for us to be open to others and to new situations while fostering optimism and cheerfulness.

Our positive or negative view of ourselves depends on self-knowledge and the fulfilment of the goals we set. To a great extent these goals take as their point of departure the role models we choose of men or women we hope to emulate. These models are presented to us in many different ways, for example through the education we receive at home, through the influence of our friends or acquaintances, and through the ideas prevalent in our particular social milieus. And so it is important to define our reference points, for if they are high and noble, they will foster a healthy self-esteem. It is also helpful to be aware of the prevailing role models in our society, as they can more or less consciously influence our own self-evaluations.

Sound role models

Sometimes we can form a distorted judgment about ourselves. We can adopt standards of success that can be unrealistic or even harmful: professional success at any price, self-centered sentimental relationships, plea-sure-based lifestyles. We might overvalue ourselves after attaining goals that some people seem to appreciate. Or the reverse is also possible: we might undervalue ourselves for not having reached certain goals or because some people don't seem to appreciate us. These mistaken appraisals are due in large measure to paying too much attention to those who evaluate people exclusively in terms of what they achieve or possess.

To avoid such risks, ask ourselves what are the reference points in our professional, family and social lives. Are these compatible with a Christian perspective? We also know that, in the end, Christ is the only complete and fully coherent model for us. Looking at our lives in light of His is the best way to evaluate ourselves, for we know that Jesus is our closest role model, with whom we have a personal and loving relationship.

Self-knowledge with God's light

If we are to judge ourselves truthfully, we need to acquire self-knowledge. This is not an easy job and is in some sense a never-ending learning process. It starts by overcoming a purely subjective perspective reflected in expressions such as "how I see things," "in my opinion," "it seems to me," making room for other considerations. If it is impossible for us to even know exactly what our own voices sound like or what our physical appearances are for others, how much more do we need to admit that we are not the best judges in assessing our own personality traits.

Besides personal reflection, self-knowledge comes from what others teach us about ourselves. This requires learning how to open up to those who can truly help us: what a wonderful means we have in personal spiritual direction! There we receive another person's advice and consider it in relation to a truly worthwhile ideal for our lives. Self-knowledge is also gained by our interactions with those around us. We have to be on guard against a superficial environment that can hinder self-reflection and make it harder to get to know ourselves truly.

Therefore we need to foster personal reflection and ask how God sees us. Prayer is the best time since getting to know God we also get to know ourselves. Among other things, we will seek his help to understand better the others' comments and advice. In some cases, we will see the need to distance ourselves from other people's judgements that are not very objective or perhaps given thoughtlessly, above all when they judge according to criteria incompatible with God's will. We need to be selective in who we pay more attention to, in keeping with what Sacred Scripture says: "It is better for a man to hear the rebuke of the wise than to hear the song of fools" (Eccl 7:5).

Moreover, since we are all partly responsible for the self-esteem of those around us, we need to do all we can to make sure our words reflect consideration for each person we encounter, seeing each as a child of God. This is especially so if we have a position of authority or guidance over others (e.g., a parent-child or teacher-student relationship, etc.), trying to ensure that our advice and suggestions help to reaffirm the conviction of their own worth, even when the need arises to correct with clarity. By doing so, we provide others with the "oxygen," the hope they need to breathe and grow on their own.

Self-acceptance: God loves us as we are

When we reflect upon our own ways of being in God's light, we are helped to accept ourselves as we are: with our talents and virtues, but also with the defects that we humbly acknowledge. True self-esteem implies recognizing that we are not all equal and that other people may be more intelligent, more musical, more athletic. . . . We all possess good qualities we can develop, and even more importantly, we are all God's children. Here lies the key to genuine self-acceptance, the positive sense of the self-esteem we need, rejecting any undue comparisons with others that could lead to sadness.

In the final analysis, we will accept ourselves as we are if we do not lose sight of the fact that God loves us with our limitations, which form part of our paths to holiness and are the raw material for our personal struggles. Our Lord chooses us, as he did the first Twelve: "ordinary men, with defects and shortcomings, more eager to say than to do. Nevertheless, Jesus calls them to be fishers of men, co-redeemers, dispensers of the grace of God."[3]

FACING SUCCESS AND FAILURE

This supernatural vantage point gives us a better grasp of our own ways of being and life story, and enables us to understand its full meaning. Temporal events and

---

3. Escrivá, *Christ Is Passing By*, no. 2.

achievements are seen in their true perspective, in the light of eternity. Thus, while happy to see we have been successful in some area, we also know that what is truly important is how it has helped us grow in holiness.

This is Christian realism, human and supernatural maturity. Just as we should not be carried away by our own successes or the praise received from others, neither should we fall into pessimism when facing failure. How much it helps us to say, with St. Peter in Acts 3:6, that anything good we have done has been done "in the name of Jesus Christ"!

At the same time, when we admit that external obstacles and our own imperfections limit our achievements, it helps shape our self-esteem, grounds personal maturity and opens the door to genuine learning. Growing in true knowledge requires recognizing our deficiencies and being ready to glean positive experiences from whatever happens to us. "You say you've failed! We never fail. You placed your confidence wholly in God. And you did not neglect any human means. Convince yourself of this truth: your success—this time—was to fail. Give thanks to our Lord, and try again!"[4] We are now ready to set out upon the way

---

4. Escrivá, *The Way*, no. 404.

of the Cross, which teaches us the paradox of strength in weakness, greatness in poverty, and growth in humiliation, with all its extraordinary effectiveness.

ACTING WITH CONFIDENCE AND A READINESS TO RECTIFY

Self-confidence is more secure when it rests on knowing we are God's beloved children and not on the certitude of attaining a success that often eludes us. This conviction enables us to accept the risk involved in any decision, to overcome the paralysis of insecurity and to be open to new situations. "A person is prudent not because he never makes a mistake, but because he corrects his errors. He shows his prudence in preferring to miss the mark twenty times rather than give in to an easy-going 'do nothing' attitude. He won't rush into things foolishly or behave with absurd rashness. He will run the risk of his decisions. Fear of failure will not make him give up in his effort to do good."[5.]

Given our human limitations and our need to grow in self-knowledge, rectifying means a personal

---

5. Escrivá, *Friends of God*, no. 88.

enrichment that leads both to an increase in our self-confidence and in our trust in those around us.

Those who entrust themselves into the hands of their heavenly Father rest secure, since "in everything God works for good with those who love him" (Rom 8:28). Even our falls are included here, when we ask God's forgiveness and with his grace get up again, growing in humility. Thus the readiness to rectify forms part of the process of conversion. "If we say we have no sin, we deceive ourselves, and the truth is not in us. If we confess our sins, he is faithful and just, and will forgive our sins and cleanse us from all unrighteousness" (1 Jn 1:8–9).

An indispensable virtue

Self-esteem ultimately flourishes under the shelter of humility, "for this is the virtue which helps us to recognize, at one and the same time, both our wretchedness and our greatness."[6] When this attitude is missing, problems related to self-esteem may easily arise. But when humility is present, it brings with it a realism that enables us to evaluate ourselves correctly. While

6. Escrivá, *Friends of God*, no. 94.

we are not impeccable, neither are we totally corrupt! We are children of God, and our shortcomings rest on an unimagined dignity.

Humility engenders an interior atmosphere that allows us to know ourselves as we truly are. And it moves us to seek sincerely the support of others and also to lend them ours. What security and trust we see in the life of Mary Most Holy! Our Lady could say that "for he who is mighty has done great things for me, and holy is his name" (Lk 1:49) because she knew very well "the low estate of his handmaiden" (Lk 1:48). In Mary, humility and knowing the greatness of her own calling are wonderfully combined.

We all need to learn from others, with an open and enriching attitude. We need the others and they need us. "If we fail to recognize the good will in others, because we cannot look into their hearts, social relationships are thrown into such discord that it becomes impossible to live alongside others."[7]

In the end, each and every one of us needs God, "for 'In him we live and move and have our being'" (Acts 17:28). He is a merciful Father who constantly watches over us, and the source and goal of our happiness, as

---

7. Augustine, *De fide rerum quae non videntur* II, 4.

St. Thérèse of Lisieux understood so well: "In the evening of this life, I shall appear before You with empty hands, for I do not ask You, Lord, to count my works. All our justice is stained in Your eyes. I wish, then, to be clothed in Your own *Justice* and to receive from Your *Love* the eternal possession of *Yourself*.[8]

---

8. Thérèse of Lisieux, "Offering to Merciful Love" (June 9, 1895).

4

Character Built on Virtue

José María Barrio and Rodolfo Valdés

THE LIFE OF GOD'S CHILDREN IS GROUNDED IN HIS GOODNESS, AND HE CALLS US TO BE VIRTUOUS.

"And as he was setting out on his journey, a man ran up and knelt before him, and asked him, 'Good Teacher, what must I do to inherit eternal life?'" (Mk 10:17). As disciples of our Lord, we witness the scene together with the Apostles—and may find ourselves surprised by his answer: "Why do you call me good? No one is good but God alone" (Mk 10:18). Jesus does not give a direct reply. With gentle divine pedagogy, he wants to lead that man to an awareness of the deepest meaning of his longing: "Jesus shows that the young man's

question is really a *religious question,* and that the goodness that attracts and at the same time obliges man
has its source in God, and indeed is God himself. God
alone is worthy of being loved 'with all one's heart, and
with all one's soul, and with all one's mind.'"[1]

To enter Life

Our Lord right away returns to that person's daring
question: what must I do? "If you would enter life," he
answers, "keep the commandments" (Mt 19:17).

The Gospels portray the young man as an obser-
vant Jew who might have been satisfied with this reply.
The Master has confirmed him in his convictions, by
pointing to the commandments he has observed since
early childhood (cf. Mk 10:20). But he wants this new
"Teacher," who speaks with authority, to spell them
out clearly. He rightly suspects that Christ can open
up for him undreamt of horizons. He asks: "Which?"
(Mt 19:18).

Jesus reminds him of the duties that have to do
with our neighbor: "You shall not kill, You shall not

---

1. John Paul II, Encyclical *Veritatis splendor* (August 6, 1993), 9.
Cf. Mt 22:37.

commit adultery, You shall not steal, You shall not bear false witness, Honor your father and mother, and, You shall love your neighbor as yourself" (Mt 19:18–19). These are the precepts of the so-called "second tablet" that safeguard "the good of the person, the image of God, by protecting his goods."[2] They are the first stage, the path towards freedom, and not yet perfect freedom, as St. Augustine remarks.[3] In other words, they are the first phase on the path of love, but not yet a mature, fully developed love.

WHAT DO I STILL LACK?

The young man knows and puts into practice these prescriptions, but his heart is asking him for more. Surely there must be something more he can do. Jesus reads his heart, and "looking upon him loved him" (Mk 10:21). Our Lord puts to him the challenge of his life: "You lack one thing; go, sell what you have, and give to the poor, and you will have treasure in heaven; and come, follow me" (Mk 10:21). Christ has placed this

---

2. John Paul II, *Veritatis splendor*, 13.

3. Cf. *In Ioannis Evangelium Tractatus*, 41, 9–10, as quoted in *Veritatis splendor*, 1.

man squarely before his own conscience, his freedom, his desire to be better. We don't know to what extent he has understood the Master's requests, although from his own question—"[W]hat do I still lack?" (Mt 19:20)—it would seem that he was expecting other "things to do." His dispositions are good, though perhaps he has not yet understood the need to interiorize the meaning of God's commandments.

The life God calls us to is not simply a question of doing good things, but of *being good*, of being virtuous.[4] Christian maturity means taking control of our lives, *asking ourselves truly*, before God, what we may still lack. We are spurred to leave the comfort zone of merely "fulfilling" the law, to discover that what really matters is following Jesus, in spite of our own mistakes. Then we will allow his teachings to transform our ways of thinking and feeling. We will experience how our hearts, which used to be small and shrunken, expands with the freedom God places there: "I will run in the way of thy commandments when thou enlargest my heart!" (Ps 119:32).

---

4. Cf. Escrivá, *The Way*, no. 337.

THE CHALLENGE
OF MORAL FORMATION

To grow in maturity means to learn to live our lives in keeping with high ideals. It is not just a matter of knowing a set of precepts, or of acquiring an ever clearer perception of the consequences of our actions. To decide to *be good*, in a word *holy*, means to identify ourselves with Christ, discovering the reasons for the way of life he offers us. Thus it requires understanding the meaning of the moral norms that teach us about the goods we should aspire to, how to attain a life that is truly fulfilled. And this is only possible if we enrich our ways of being with the Christian virtues.

PILLARS OF CHARACTER

Moral knowledge is not an abstract discourse, nor a technique. The formation of a moral conscience requires a strengthening of character that is grounded on the virtues as its pillars. Virtues reinforce our personalities, rendering it stable and even-tempered. They enable us to rise above ourselves, our self-centeredness, and focus our concern on God and others. A virtuous person is "poised," with the right measure in all things, upright, self-possessed and well-rounded. Those who are short on virtue, in contrast, will find it hard to undertake significant projects or to give shape to high ideals. They will be forever improvising and lurching to and fro and end up being unreliable, even for themselves.

Fostering virtues enlarges our freedom. Virtue has nothing to do with getting used to situations or acting out of routine. To be sure, a single action is not enough for a good operative habit to take root, to shape our ways of being and make it easier for us to do good. Habits are formed thanks to repeated actions: we become good by *being* good. To act once and again upon the resolution of getting down to study at a set time, for example, renders every successive effort a little less costly. But we need to persevere in this effort in order to preserve the habit of study, or otherwise it might be lost.

RENEWING THE SPIRIT

Virtues, both human and supernatural, direct us towards the good, towards the attainment of our deepest aspirations. They help us reach true happiness, union with God: "And this is eternal life, that they know thee the only true God, and Jesus Christ whom thou hast sent" (Jn 17:3). They make it easier to act in accord with moral precepts. Virtues are no longer seen as rules to follow but as a path leading to Christian perfection, to identification with Christ in the life marked out by the beatitudes. The beatitudes, a portrait of Christ's face, "speak of basic attitudes and dispositions in life"[5] that lead us to eternal life.

The path of growth in Christian life then opens up before us, as St. Paul exhorts: "[B]e transformed by the renewal of your mind, that you may prove what is the will of God, what is good and acceptable and perfect" (Rom 12:2). Grace transforms the ways we judge events and gives us new criteria for action. We gradually learn to adjust our ways of seeing things to God's will, expressed also in the moral law. And then we come to love moral goodness, a holy life, and taste "what is good and acceptable and perfect" (Rom 12:2). We reach Christian maturity in our moral and emotional lives, which helps us to readily grasp what is noble, true, just and beautiful, and to reject sin, which offends the dignity of God's children.

---

5. John Paul II, *Veritatis splendor*, 16.

This path leads to the forging, as St. Josemaría said, of a "person of sound judgment."[6] But what are the characteristics of this sound judgment? Elsewhere he says that it "requires maturity, firm convictions, sufficient doctrinal knowledge, a refined spirit and an educated will."[7] An excellent portrait of a Christian personality! We need the *maturity* required to make decisions with interior freedom and to take responsibility for them. Also firm and sure *convictions*, based on a deep knowledge of Christian doctrine. Convictions are acquired through formational classes or talks, reading good books, reflection, and especially through the good example given by others, since "the true guiding stars of our life are the people who have lived good lives."[8] And along with this, a *refined spirit*, shown in kindness towards others, and an *educated will* that leads to a virtuous life. A "person of sound judgment," therefore, will ask in every circumstance: What does God expect of me? He or she will ask the Holy Spirit for light, have recourse to the principles they have assimilated, seek advice from those able to help, and act in consequence.

---

6. Escrivá, *The Way*, no. 33.

7. Escrivá, *Conversations*, no. 93.

8. Benedict XVI, Encyclical *Spe salvi* (November 30, 2007), 49.

FRUIT OF LOVE

Thus moral behavior, specified in living out the commandments under the impetus of the virtues, stems from love, which spurs us to seek and foster moral goodness. This love is much more than just feelings, which by their very nature are fluctuating and fleeting. It does not depend on our moods or what we like or would prefer to do in a given situation. Rather, to love and be loved means to give ourselves, in a self-giving grounded on the awareness that we are loved by God, and on the high ideals that are worth staking our freedom on: "When people give themselves freely, at every moment of their self-surrender, freedom renews their love; to be renewed in that way is to be always young, generous, capable of high ideals and great sacrifices."[9]

Christian perfection is not restricted to fulfilling a set of rules, nor to striving for isolated goals such as self-control or efficiency. Rather it leads to surrendering our freedom to our Lord, responding to his invitation with the help of his grace: ". . . come, follow me" (Mk 10:21). It is about living according to the Spirit, (cf. Gal 5:16) impelled by charity, with the desire to

---

9. Escrivá, *Friends of God*, no. 31.

serve others. And then we come to understand that God's law is the privileged path for putting into practice this freely chosen love. Rather than rules, it is a question of adhering to Jesus, of sharing in his life and destiny, in loving obedience to his Father's will.

Avoiding "perfectionism"

The determination to grow in maturity by strengthening the virtues is far removed from a narcissistic quest for perfection. We struggle out of love for our Father God, with our gaze fixed on Him, not on ourselves. Therefore we need to reject any tendency to "perfectionism" that might arise were we to focus our inner struggle in terms of efficiency or results. While such an approach may be quite common in certain professional environments, it disfigures the Christian moral life. Holiness lies above all in loving God.

Maturity leads to harmonizing the desire to act uprightly with the real limitations that we experience in ourselves and in others. We may sometimes feel inclined to make St. Paul's words our own: "I do not understand my own actions. For I do not do what I want, but I do the very thing I hate. . . . Wretched man that I am! Who will deliver me from this body of death?" (Rom 7:15, 24). We won't lose our peace, though, since God tells us, as he did the Apostle: "My grace is sufficient for you" (2 Cor 12:9). Our gratitude and hope grow stronger, since God takes our limitations into account, as long as they spur us to convert our lives and to approach Him for help.

Here, too, Christians find a firm reference point in Jesus' first reply to that young man: "One there is who is good" (Mt 19:17). The life of God's children is grounded in his goodness. He gives us the strength to direct our whole lives towards what is truly valuable, to understand what is good and to love it, in order to render ourselves fit for the mission He has entrusted to us.

5

Building Interior Order

José Benito Cabaniña and Carlos Ayxelá

CHRISTIAN CONSISTENCY—FRUIT OF A RICH
INNER LIFE—ENABLES US TO DEDICATE OURSELVES
TO AN IDEAL.

When St. Augustine, towards the end of his life, wrote
the words "the peace of all things is the tranquility
of order,"[1] he did so with the experience of one who
for years had felt the constant tug of many different
demands: the pastoral care of the portion of the People
of God entrusted to him; his abundant preaching; the
challenges of unsettled times, with changes in society
and culture. So this was not an adage written amid a
calm retirement, but rather in the hustle and bustle of

---

1. Augustine, *The City of God*, XIX, 13.1.

daily life, with all its unpredictable demands. The unified life of this saint was a daily conquest. Over time, his steady effort to "aim at the target" led in the end to a strong character.

One of the traits of a mature personality is the ability to combine intense activity with order and interior peace. Achieving this equilibrium requires real effort. For grace and the supernatural virtues to take deep root and heal every corner of our lives, they need to be received in a noble, natural "vessel." Human virtues such as industriousness, prudence, maturity, and sincerity thus welcome the divine treasure God offers us. Little by little the divine and human are integrated into a "unity of life" that reflects the unity between the human and divine natures in Christ, our Model.

Order, the harmony in our lives, is a prize we have to win, bit by bit, on the battlefield of each day. "[B]eginning the least pleasant but most urgent job first, . . . perseverance in the fulfillment of our duty when it would be easy to abandon it, not leaving for tomorrow what should be finished today: and all this, to please him, our Father God!"[2]

---

2. Escrivá, *Friends of God*, no. 67.

Self-mastery

This serene struggle is not just about our exterior actions and the tasks that fill our days, but also about our hearts. Without that inner heartbeat, order would only be time-management, "task optimization," cold efficiency, and not an authentic exercise of Christian maturity. Christian consistency is built on a constant flow, from the inside to the outside and from the outside to the inside. It grows with self-mastery, order in one's exterior activities, inner recollection and prudence.

We are not unaware of the obstacles against achieving this interior harmony. While we appreciate the great attractiveness of a fully Christian life, we often feel different, and sometimes contrary, tendencies. St. Paul expressed this forcefully: "So I find it to be a law that when I want to do right, evil lies close at hand. For I delight in the law of God, in my inmost self, but I see in my members another law at war with the law of my mind and making me captive to the law of sin which dwells in my members" (Rom 7:21–23). We know something is good, yet we feel attracted to something else. We are aware of being divided between what attracts us and what we should do, which can end up clouding our vision. It might even seem to us that, when all is said and done, it won't matter if we are a bit inconsistent—a clear sign of a wavering love.

Nevertheless, our Lord's praise for Nathaniel resounds in our hearts: "Behold, an Israelite indeed, in whom is no guile!" (Jn 1:47). Those who strive to be guided by God's voice echoing in their conscience spontaneously inspire great respect. People with an undivided heart are attractive, because everything in them speaks of authenticity. In contrast, a double life, big or small actions contrary to a person's values or commitments, and a lack of sincerity mar the beauty of a soul. As we are all prey to these small deviations, it's a matter of acting with simplicity and correcting them with perseverance.

PLAYING GOD'S MELODY

Putting our inner lives in order is not just a matter of our intellect "dominating" our imagination and channeling the force of our feelings and sentiments. We need to discover everything that these travelling companions in life can and want to tell us. In other words, we cannot correct the dissonance by suppressing one of the melodies: God has made us "polyphonic." Self-mastery, also called temperance, is not cerebral frigidity. God wants us to have a heart that is "big and strong and tender, affectionate and refined."[3]

We can, as it were, play music for God with our hearts. But to play it well we need to tune it properly, just as instruments are tuned in order to sound the right note. We need to educate our affections, developing a sensitivity for what is really good because it is in accord with all the dimensions of our beings as persons. Our feelings give color to our whole lives and allow us to perceive what happens around us with greater depth. Nevertheless, just as a canvas with unbalanced colors is not very attractive, or a musical instrument out of tune is bothersome, so a heart abandoned to the vagaries of sentiment disrupts the harmony of our personalities and erodes our relations with others, sometimes seriously.

St. Josemaría advised people to lock their heart with "seven bolts."[4] As he once explained: "lock it with

---

3. Escrivá, *Friends of God*, no. 177.
4. Escrivá, *The Way*, nos. 161, 188.

the seven bolts that I recommend: one for each of the capital sins. But don't give up having a heart."[5] The accumulated experience of past centuries, also in parts of the world where Christianity has not yet arrived, shows that the affections and instincts, if not controlled, can drag us along like floodwaters that sweep away whatever they touch. It's not a matter of stopping the flow, but of doing what engineers do who channel the torrent rushing down the mountainside to power turbines that produce electricity. Once the torrent that might have uprooted trees and demolished houses is channeled, everyone can live peacefully and benefit. If our spirits fail to channel in a stable way the instinctive and affective impulses of our human nature, we cannot have peace or calm, nor can interior life exist.

Taking Charge of Our Day

An important step towards self-mastery is the effort to overcome laziness, a silent but effective "virus"

---

5. Josemaría Escrivá notes taken at a get-together in Santiago, Chile, on June 30, 1974. "These sins are called 'capital' because they engender other sins, other vices. They are pride, avarice, envy, wrath, lust, gluttony and sloth or acedia" (*Catechism of the Catholic Church*, 1866).

which could little by little paralyze us if we do not keep it in line. Laziness takes root in someone who has no clear direction in life, or who, knowing such a direction, doesn't follow it. "Don't confuse serenity with being lazy or careless, with putting off decisions or deferring the study of important matters."[6] Concentrating on matters that need our attention, confronting something that requires a bit of effort, not leaving for later what we can do now—on these habits one can readily build an agile, strong and serene personality.

We should also be wary of the other extreme, disordered activism. "[D]o not busy yourself with many matters. . . . There is a man who works, and toils, and presses on, but is so much the more in want" (Sir 11:10–11). A mature personality means pondering things, putting order into our activity. Then life will not overwhelm us with its unlimited demands. Rather we will take the initiative by distributing our activities among the time available. By planning our days, without being too rigid, we can give priority to what should take first place, rather than whatever arises. Thus we will prevent what seems urgent from replacing what is

---

6. Escrivá, *The Forge*, no. 467.

really important. Of course it is not necessary to program everything, but we should avoid the improvisation that leads to wasting time simply because we get involved in whatever happens during the day.

Each day contains certain key moments that we can decide on beforehand: the time to go to bed, the time to get up, the time we are going to dedicate exclusively to God, the time to work, times for meals, and so on. Then, we will do very well all those things we need to do, working hard and as well as we can, that is, working with love. "Carry out the little duty of each moment: do what you ought and concentrate on what you are doing."[7] This is, in the end, a program for holiness that does not shackle us, because it is ordered to a great end: to please God and make others happy. At the same time, the very love that leads us to subject ourselves to a timetable will tell us when this plan needs to be set aside, because the good of others requires it, or for other good reasons that become clear to anyone living in the presence of God.

---

7. Escrivá, *The Way*, no. 815.

Nurturing interior space

The interior world of the person is the vital center, where one's strengths, qualities, dispositions and actions form a unity. Whoever is able to reside there, to recollect the senses and faculties and quiet the soul, will develop a richer personality, more capable of relating to others and dialoguing with them. "Silence," said Benedict XVI, "is an integral element of communication; in its absence, words rich in content cannot exist."[8]

To avoid skimming along the surface of life, we need to spend time reflecting on what has happened to us, on the books we have read, on what others have told us, and above all on the lights we have received from God. Reflection broadens and enriches our interior spaces and helps us to integrate work, social relations, leisure, etc. into the plan of Christian life. This habit implies that we learn to enter into our souls, overcoming haste, impatience and dispersion. Thus a space for meditating in God's presence will open up. "'Who among us . . . in the evening, before the day is over, is alone' and 'asks himself' [W]hat has happened

---

8. Benedict XVI, *Message for the 46th World Communications Day* (May 20, 2012).

in my heart today? What has occurred? What things have passed through my heart?"[9]

This calmness of spirit is achieved when we cut ourselves off from the tensions of life and pause on the demands of pending matters, when we slow down the rhythm of exterior life and we are quiet exteriorly as well as interiorly. Then our knowledge and experience acquire depth; we learn to be surprised, to contemplate, to savor the riches of the spirit, to listen to God. When we go out to others with this interior richness, we can enjoy communicating with them more, since we have something personal, something of *our own*, to contribute.

In silence, we can hear God's voice. When the Lord wanted to pass by Elijah on Mount Horeb, Sacred Scripture tells us that he was not in the violent wind that shattered the boulders, nor in the fearful earthquake, nor in the fire that followed, but in the gentle breeze that could hardly be detected (cf. 1 Kgs 19:11–13). Silence is beautiful; it is not emptiness but an authentic and full

---

9. Pope Francis, Morning Meditation in the Chapel of Domus Sanctae Marthae (October 10, 2014), as quoted in "The Heart on Guard," *L'Osservatore Romano*, Weekly ed. in English, n. 42 (17 October 2014). *https://w2.vatican.va/content/francesco/en/cotidie/2014/documents/papa-francesco-cotidie_20141010_the-heart-on-guard.html*.

life if it allows one to establish an intimate dialogue with
God. "The tuneful sound of silence: in this way we can
approach God, since the melody of silence is something
proper to people in love."[10]

Wisdom of the heart

"The wise of heart is called a man of discernment"
(Prv 16:21).

The capacity for recollection allows us to establish
with ever greater depth the motives that guide our lives.

We don't always need to give an immediate
response to what we confront. Often prudence will
lead us to seek further information before making a
judgment or taking a decision, because things are often
not as they appear at first glance. A mature person is
characterized by considering matters attentively, recall-
ing past experiences of similar situations, and seeking
trustworthy advice. And above all, something that for
a Christian seems very natural, almost a reflex: seeking
advice from God. "Never make a decision without stopping to consider the matter in the presence of God."[11]
Thus it is easier to apply to the particular situation a

10. Pope Francis, Homily (December 12, 2013).

11. Escrivá, *The Way*, no. 266.

judgment that has been carefully considered, without giving in to superficiality, to comfort-seeking, to bad habits from the past, or to pressure from our surroundings. And we will find the courage needed to make a decision and to carry it out without delay, with the readiness to rectify if later on we realize that we have made a mistake.

Christian consistency enables us to dedicate ourselves to an ideal and to persevere in it. The clouds of a darkened or obscured vision will sooner or later dissipate. Steadily seeking the goal we have set for ourselves in life is a daily task, perhaps the most important one. It is a conquest filled with beauty. A French writer, born in a humble peasant family and who was self-taught, defined faith in this way: "Never denying when darkness comes what one has seen clearly in the light."[12] Here God enables us to imitate Him, since He is always faithful.

---

12. Gustave Thibon, *Entre el amor y la muerte* (Madrid: Rialp, 1977), p. 35.

6

A Life in Dialogue with Others

Alfonso Aguiló

WE DIALOGUE IN ORDER TO LEARN

"The kiln tests the potter's vessels; so the test of a person is in his conversation. The fruit discloses the cultivation of a tree; so the expression of a thought discloses the cultivation of a man's mind" (Sir 27:5–7). An essential sign of human maturity is the ability to dialogue. An attitude of openness towards others is shown by cordial dealings and a sincere desire to learn from each person.

"Becoming acquainted with other people and other cultures is always good for us; it makes us grow. . . . Dialogue is very important for our own maturity, because in confronting another person, confronting other cultures, and also confronting other religions in the right way, we grow; we develop and mature. There is of course a danger. If during dialogue someone closes himself in and grows angry he may start a fight. There is the danger of conflict and this is not good, because we talk to each other to explain ourselves and not in order to quarrel. And what is the deepest approach we should have in order to dialogue and not quarrel? Meekness, the ability to encounter people, to encounter cultures peacefully; the ability to ask intelligent questions: 'But why do you think like this? Why does this culture do this?' Listening to others and then speaking. First listening, then speaking."[1]

Knowing how to listen

Sacred Scripture amply praises those who are ready to listen, while scorning the attitude of those who pay no heed to others. "He whose ear heeds wholesome admonition will abide among the wise" (Prv 15:31), says the book of Proverbs. The Apostle James advises us to "be quick to hear, slow to speak, slow to anger" (Jas 1:19).

---

1. Francis, Address to Students and Teachers from the Seibu Gakuen Bunri Junior High School of Saitama, Tokyo (August 21, 2013).

A frequent problem in listening is that, while another person is speaking, we recall something related to what that person is saying, and we are eager to have "our say" as soon as a pause occurs. Then conversations ensue that perhaps are spirited, but with constant interruptions. Little real listening takes place.

Sometimes the problem is that conversation does not arise spontaneously, and we need to be clever in trying to bring it about. In such cases presumption needs to be avoided. That is the tendency to make a show of our own insights and knowledge. On the contrary, it is good to show that we are open and receptive, eager to learn from others, and thus to steadily widen our range of interests.

Perhaps first we have to break the ice that can make communication difficult. Opportune questions can open up a current of interest with the person we are dialoguing with. Then we will listen attentively to topics that perhaps at first do not greatly attract us. This does not imply hypocrisy on our part, but rather the sincere effort to rise above our own points of view and to learn from others.

The ability to start up a conversation requires both daring and prudence, interest in others and discretion, risk and appropriate remarks. We can't speak off the top of our heads. We need to be ready to undo any hasty or inappropriate words we may have uttered unthinkingly, or amend a strong statement that we should have pondered more carefully. In any case, good conversations always leave a mark. The ideas and trains of thought expressed on both sides come to mind later on and result in new insights, along with an eagerness to continue that exchange.

Openness to others

It is surprising to see how some people seem to grow old prematurely in their interior attitudes; while others remain young at heart and open right to the end of their days. The fact is that we all carry within ourselves many untapped reserves. These include talents we have not yet taken advantage of and strengths we have never tested. So no matter how busy or tired we may be, we cannot allow ourselves to stop progressing, and need to learn from others and be receptive to new ideas.

Getting out of ourselves is good for us. We open ourselves to God and to others through him. Thus we overcome the self-centeredness that sometimes leads us to try to make reality accord with our own narrow interests or viewpoints. And we will be more on guard against personal shortcomings that can create distances between people, and that are a sign of immaturity. For example, expressing opinions with a dogmatic certainty that often doesn't align with our true knowledge of things, or in a way that implies a veiled criticism of others. Other signs of immaturity are making use of "pre-fabricated" solutions or repetitive and trite pieces of advice; becoming irritated when someone doesn't think the way we do, even though we claim to support variety and tolerance; being filled with jealousy when someone we know excels us; demanding from others a level of perfection that is beyond them, and us; and expecting people to be open and sincere, when we ourselves resist being corrected.

MATURITY AND CORRECTING OTHERS

When we look upon others with affection, we will often notice how we can help them with friendly advice. We will tell them in confidence what others have perhaps seen but did not have the loyalty to tell them. For our correction and criticism to be useful and constructive, it has to stem from charity: "when you have to correct, you should do so with charity, at the opportune moment, without humiliating. And being ready yourself to learn and to improve in the very faults you are correcting."[2]

The key to helping others change is in a certain sense linked to our own abilities to change and improve in our own lives. When we appreciate how hard it is for us to change and improve, and yet how important and liberating is that effort, then we find it easier to see others objectively and help them. Those who can speak the truth clearly to themselves will know how and when to do so with others, and will be open to listening to others who tell them things clearly.

Being able to receive and accept criticism is proof of spiritual depth and wisdom. Nevertheless, accepting what others tell us does not mean being influenced by every possible criticism of our professional or social affairs. If we "danced to every tune" that others raise about what we are or do, we would worry ourselves sick. At times people who are working for the good are much criticized. Sometimes it is by those who themselves are doing very little, and who see the good lives and work of others as an indictment of their own (cf. Wis 2:10–20). Other times, a person of virtue may be

2. Escrivá, *The Forge*, no. 455.

viewed as an "enemy" by those who act differently. And even those who carry out the same or similar deeds may criticize out of jealousy. At times we may have to "pardon" others who are doing practically nothing themselves, or those who cannot imagine anything good being accomplished without them.

THE RESPONSIBILITY OF GIVING GOOD EXAMPLE

Maturity unites openness to others with fidelity to one's path and principles, even when scarcely an echo of support comes from the surrounding environment. Any indifference we encounter could also be an indication that we ourselves need to change in some area, or to learn how to explain or present things better. But there are some core principles that we should never change, no matter what happens. Regardless of whether people listen to us or not, praise or insult us, thank or reject us, approve or disapprove: "and that contrast—because you're confirming your faith with works—is exactly the naturalness I ask of you."[3]

---

3. Escrivá, *The Way*, no. 380.

It is not unusual for a person to feel alone and unaided when undertaking great endeavors. The temptation then to give up can be very strong. Someone might even think that their example and witness is of little value. But this isn't so; perhaps a match cannot light up a whole room, but everyone in the room can see the light. Perhaps many people feel incapable of following the example being given, but in their heart of hearts they would like to, and thus are stirred to aim for higher goals.

We can all recall how much the good example of so many people has helped us to improve. And yet most of these people probably don't realize the effect they've had on our lives. We have a big responsibility to try to exert a positive influence on others. We need to speak, give advice, exhort and encourage others. But above all we must back up our words with deeds, through the testimony of our own life. While it is impossible for us to always do so, we should aim at assisting everyone, and ask sincerely for forgiveness if we have failed in some way.

DEVELOPING OUR OWN CRITERIA

Deciding on our personal criteria and standards is never an easy task. We have at hand so much information that we have ready access to, but the important thing is not having a great quantity of data but knowing if it is reliable and how to act on it, seeing interconnections and drawing out from this data true knowledge.

The key to developing sound criteria, to having prudence and maturity in evaluating events and making decisions, lies not in knowing many things but in a practical wisdom. One of the means for acquiring it is reading good books, combined with the ability to question and observe life closely. Another important means is not allowing oneself to be overly influenced by current fads and ways of acting. Many people think they have developed a way of thinking and a lifestyle that is all their own, totally personal and original, when in reality they think and do and consume what others have designed for everyone else and consume.

Our learning, our dialogue with the world, never ends. We have to never give up studying, and being unsatisfied by the explanations that others give us (and that we give ourselves). We need to be determined to continue learning from both young and old, from those who know much or little, from those we like and those we don't, those who agree with our ideas and those who challenge them. We have to be open to everyone, and respect those who think differently than we do, with a great desire to learn from them, while being faithful to our faith and personal values. Thus we won't dilute the truth or lose the courage needed to seek it, love it and live it with all its consequences.

A LIFELONG BATTLE

Openness to others is closely united to our progress in the lifelong battle to unmask the face of pride and grow in humility. Pride seeps into the most surprising nooks and crannies of our relationships with others. Were it to rear its ugly head openly, we would see how repulsive it is; so one of its most typical subterfuges is to conceal or mask its face. Pride often hides itself under another, seemingly positive trait, which it subtly contaminates. And when pride has set down deep roots, its simpler and more basic manifestations appear, signs of an immature personality: an unhealthy oversensitivity; constantly speaking about oneself; vanity and affectation in one's gestures and way of speaking; an arrogant or conceited attitude, combined with deep discouragement upon perceiving one's own weaknesses.

Sometimes pride can disguise itself as wisdom, with an intellectual pride shown in the need to always be rigorously right. At other times it hides behind a passionate zeal for justice and defence of the truth, under which lie the desire to "get back at" others, or an arrogant "orthodoxy" that seeks to dominate them. What one is really seeking is to control everything, to be the judge of everything. These are attitudes that, instead of serving the truth, make use of it to stay on top of others.

Just as there is no such thing as perfect health, neither can we ever completely escape from the sophistries of pride. However, we can learn to detect it more readily so it does not gain more ground in our souls. At times, inevitably, we are fooled by pride, since it tends to entrench itself in us, and we become reluctant to let others help us see our defects. But even if we do not see pride's face, hidden in so many ways, perhaps others can see it more clearly. If we are willing to listen to their fraternal warning, their constructive criticism, it will be much easier for us to unmask it. We need to be humble in order to accept the help of the others. And we also need to be humble if we are to help others without humiliating them in turn.

The personality God wants for us (to which we all aspire, albeit erringly at times) is that of someone who has "a heart that loves, a heart that suffers, a heart that rejoices with others."[4]

---

4. Francis, Address to Participants in the Ecclesial Convention (June 17, 2013).

7

Sharing Others' Feelings

Javier Laínez

Empathy is not a strategy or a technique, but rather love for the truth.

We have all had the experience that simply being told dry facts often fails to satisfy our desires to grasp what is going on in the world. For example, someone who plays a piece of music to entertain friends surely hopes that they will enjoy listening to it as much as he or she does in playing it. But if the friends listening simply say that the musical piece has been well executed, without showing the slightest enthusiasm, then the likely result will be discouragement.

How many problems could be avoided if we truly tried to understand better others' feelings, their expectations and ideals. "Charity consists not so much in giving as in understanding."[1] The first requirement of charity is recognizing in the other person someone worthy of consideration and placing ourselves in that person's circumstances. The word "empathy" is often used to refer to the ability to put oneself in other people's shoes, taking stock of their situation and being aware of their sentiments. Joined to charity, this attitude fosters communion, the union of hearts. As St. Peter exhorted: "have unity of spirit, sympathy, love of the brethren, a tender heart" (1Pet 3:8).

LEARNING FROM CHRIST

Right from the start the disciples experienced how sensitive Christ was to those around him: his ability to put himself in the place of others, his refined understanding of what was going on inside the human heart, his sensitivity to the suffering of others. On reaching Nain, without a word being spoken, he realizes the heartbreak of the widow who has lost her only son (cf. Lk 7:11–17). On hearing Jairus' petition and the laments of the mourners, he brings consolation to the first and calm to the others (cf. Lk 8:40–56; Mt 9:18–26). He is aware of the needs of those following

---

1. Escrivá, *The Way*, no. 463.

him and is concerned when they have nothing to eat (cf. Mt 15:32). He cries with Martha and Mary before Lazarus' tomb (cf. Jn 11:35) and becomes indignant at his followers' hardness of heart when they want to call down fire from heaven upon the Samaritan village that refused to receive them (cf. Lk 9:51–56).

By his life Jesus teaches us to see others in a different way, to share their feelings and accompany them in their hopes and disappointments. We learn from him to take an interest in the interior world of those around us, and with the help of grace we gradually overcome defects such as distraction, impulsiveness, or coldness. There is no excuse for giving up in this effort. "Remember that even if your virtues seem saintly, they are worth nothing if they are not united to the ordinary Christian virtues."[2] Being close to our Lord's Heart will help mold our hearts and fill it with the sentiments of Christ Jesus.

CHARITY, AFFABILITY AND EMPATHY

"The charity of Christ is not merely a benevolent sentiment for our neighbor; it is not limited to a

---

2. Escrivá, *The Way*, no. 409.

penchant for philanthropy. Poured out in our souls by God, charity transforms from within our minds and will. It provides the supernatural foundation for friendship and the joy of doing what is right."[3] The apostles, through their close relationship with our Lord, learn to moderate their quite diverse temperaments, which sometimes had led them to scorn others. John, so vehement that he merited with his brother James the nickname "son of thunder," later saw his heart filled with meekness and insisted on the need to open our hearts to our neighbors and give ourselves to others as Christ did: "By this we know love, that he laid down his life for us; and we ought to lay down our lives for the brethren" (1 Jn 3:16).

St. Peter, who also had shown harshness towards Christ's adversaries in the past, addresses the people in the Temple with words devoid of any rancor, seeking their conversion: "And now, brethren, I know that you acted in ignorance, as did also your rulers. . . . Repent therefore, and turn again, that your sins may be blotted out, that times of refreshing may come from the presence of the Lord" (Acts 3:17,19–20).

---

3. Escrivá, *Christ Is Passing By*, no. 71.

We see another example in St. Paul. After being a fierce scourge to Christians, he converts and places at the service of the gospel his clear mind and strong character. In Athens, although his heart is indignant at seeing so many idols, he strives to empathize with the inhabitants. When he has occasion to address them on the Areopagus, instead of taking them to task for their paganism and depraved morals, he appeals to their hunger for God: "'Men of Athens, I perceive that in every way you are very religious. For as I passed along, and observed the objects of your worship, I found also an altar with this inscription, "To an unknown god." What therefore you worship as unknown, this I proclaim to you'" (Acts 17:22–23). In the Apostle Paul's ability to understand and inspire others, we see a person who can integrate and moderate his emotions. He shows the cordiality needed to grasp the situation others are in and focus on a perhaps quite small but positive aspect of their mentality, in order to connect with his hearers, capture their interest and lead them to the fullness of the truth.

PATHS TOWARDS LOVING THE TRUTH

In trying to help others, charity and kindness will guide us to the "reasons of the heart" that often open the doors of the soul more easily than do cold and distant arguments. God's love spurs us to an affable way of being that shows the attractiveness of Christian life. "True virtue is not sad and repulsive, but pleasantly joyful."[4] We learn to discover positive aspects in each person, since loving the truth entails recognizing God's footprints, however faint, in others' hearts.

In dealing with friends, work colleagues and relatives, charity leads us to show understanding towards those who are disorientated, at times because they have not had the opportunity to receive good formation in the faith, or because that have not met a person incarnating the authentic Gospel message. Thus empathy is possible even when others are in error. "I do not understand violence. I do not consider it a proper way either to persuade or to win over. Error is overcome by prayer, by God's grace, and by study; never by force, always with charity."[5]

We have to speak the truth with unfailing love, *veritatem facientes in caritate*, (cf. Eph 4:15) accompanying those who may be confused, but who over time can open themselves to the action of grace. As Pope

---

4. Escrivá, *The Way*, no. 657.

5. Escrivá, *Conversations*, no. 44.

Francis said, "Often it is better simply to slow down, to put aside our eagerness in order to see and listen to others, to stop rushing from one thing to another and to remain with someone who has faltered along the way. At times we have to be like the father of the prodigal son, who always keeps his door open so that when the son returns, he can readily pass through it."[6]

APOSTOLATE AND COMMUNION OF SENTIMENTS

Some people could try to reduce empathy to a simple strategy, as though it were a technique used to sell a consumer product, to make people think it is just what they were looking for. Although this might be valid in a commercial context, interpersonal relations follow a different logic. Authentic empathy requires sincerity and is incompatible with behavior that masks self-interest.

Sincerity is vital in seeking to make our Lord known to those around us. By making our own the sentiments of the people God has placed at our sides, we will have the refined charity needed to share in

---

6. Francis, Apostolic Exhortation *Evangelii Gaudium* (November 24, 2013), 46.

each one's joy and sorrow. "Who is weak, and I am not weak? Who is made to fall, and I am not indignant?" (2 Cor 11:29). What sincere affection is reflected in these words of St. Paul to the Christians at Corinth. It is easier for truth to open a pathway when we share in others' sentiments, because a current of affection, of cordiality, is opened that reinforces communication. The soul becomes more receptive to the advice received, especially if a constructive comment is made that encourages growth in that person's spiritual life.

"Listening, in communication, is an openness of heart which makes possible that closeness without which genuine spiritual encounter cannot occur. Listening helps us to find the right gesture and word which shows that we are more than simply bystanders."[7] When we listen attentively we get involved intimately in the lives of others. We seek to help the other person discern the specific steps God is asking at this particular moment. And when others sense that their situation, opinions and sentiments are respected, and even shared in by the one listening, they open the eyes of their soul to contemplate the splendor of truth, the attractiveness of virtue.

---

7. Pope Francis, *Evangelii Gaudium*, 171.

In contrast, indifference is a serious defect for an apostolic soul. We cannot be distant from those around us: "People who think you are unpleasant will stop thinking that when they realize you really love them. It is up to you."[8] Our words filled with understanding, our small deeds of service, our friendly conversations reflect a sincere interest in the welfare of the people beside us. We will learn how to win the affection of others, opening the door to a friendship that shares with them the marvelous reality of dealing closely with God.

ENCOURAGING OTHERS TO SET OUT

Pope Francis counseled that "[s]omeone good at such accompaniment does not give in to frustrations or fears. He or she invites others to let themselves be healed, to take up their mat, embrace the cross, leave all behind and go forth ever anew to proclaim the Gospel."[9] On getting to know others' weaknesses we also encourage them not to give in to conformity, to widen their horizons so that they continue aspiring to reach the goal of sanctity.

---

8. Escrivá, *Furrow*, no. 734.

9. Pope Francis, *Evangelii Gaudium*, 172.

By acting in this way, we will follow our Lord's example, being very understanding while also making affectionate demands on people. On Easter Sunday afternoon, when walking beside the disciples from Emmaus, Jesus asked them: "What is this conversation which you are holding with each other as you walk?" (Lk 24:17). He lets them unburden themselves of the disillusion weighing on their hearts and the difficulty they had in believing Jesus had really returned to life, as the holy women had testified. Only then does our Lord explain to them the meaning of what has happened: "Was it not necessary that the Christ should suffer these things and enter into his glory?" (Lk 24:26).

What must Jesus' conversation have been like, how much must his words have eased the worries of the disciples from Emmaus, for them to say at the end: "Stay with us" (Lk 24:29)? And they do so despite the fact that initially he reproached them for their inability to grasp what the prophets had announced (cf. Lk 24:25). Perhaps it was his tone of voice, his affectionate look, that made them feel welcomed, but at the same time invited them to change. With God's grace our dealings with others will also show appreciation for each person, a real understanding of what is going on in each one's heart, thus encouraging them to set out on the path of Christian life.

8

Growth:
A Family Project

Wenceslao Vial

GRANDPARENTS, PARENTS, CHILDREN
AND GRANDCHILDREN ARE ALL CALLED TO GIVE
THE BEST OF THEMSELVES

How she resembles her mother! The same smile, the same hand gestures when talking, even the same way of walking! Often we hear or make comments like these. For it's true that we acquire many characteristics of the personality of our parents and siblings, without even realizing it. Some characteristics are inherited, like the color of our eyes, our temperaments, or our ways of being. But many others have been forged by our daily dealings and encounters with others, by our formation—in a word, by life itself.

The characteristics of personal maturity that we have dealt with in the preceding chapters are sown and grow in the context of the family. Therefore, how important it is to take good care of the family! It is and should be the fertile soil in which our paths begin, develop and finish. "In reality, it is a motive of great joy to feel at every stage of life, in every situation, in every social condition, that we are and remain sons and daughters."[1]

The responsibility for the family, as willed by God, binds us all, whether as parents or brothers and sisters—and at the same time always as sons and daughters. We will consider our roles in the home in two stages. First, we will reflect in this chapter on what makes the family unique, and on the "job" of parents and children. In the next chapter we will delve more deeply into family life and the aspects that fill it with light and joy. "Today, more important than the pastoral care of failures is the pastoral effort to strengthen marriages and thus to prevent their breakdown."[2]

---

1. Francis, General Audience (March 18, 2015).

2. Francis, *Amoris laetitia*, 307.

Giving our best in the home means giving everything

Each person has his or her own history, the imprint left on our lives by so many different situations, whether joyful or painful. Our past is also framed within God's plans, which are sometimes mysterious for us. There are homes in which Christian example has been lacking, although sooner or later the figure of Christ has ended up being glimpsed in a friend, a relative or a teacher. In many other families we see the affectionate effort to raise the children in the faith, along with the defects and limitations of parents and siblings.

We have not chosen our family members, but God has. He counted not only on their virtues, but also on their defects in order to make us Christians: "In the family, and we are all witnesses of this, miracles are performed with what little we have, with what we are, with what is at hand... and many times, it is not the ideal, it is not what we dreamt of, nor what 'should have been.'"[3]

All of us—grandparents, parents, children and grandchildren—are called to give the best of

---

3. Francis, Homily at Holy Mass for Families, Guayaquil (July 6, 2015).

ourselves at every moment, with God's help, in order to impart a Christian tone to our families. Parents also grow with their children, and, with the passage of the years, family roles can interchange. The one who guided others before is now guided; the one who led cedes this responsibility to those coming after. The home formed by everyone is much more than the primary resource for the basic necessities of nutrition, warmth, and clothing. Along with all that, it is the place where we discover the beauty of authentic human values; of self-control and respect, so necessary for interpersonal relationships;[4] of responsibility, loyalty and a spirit of service. All these values are forged in a slow fire that requires a simple but strong sense of belonging: the awareness of not having been simply "thrown" into the world, but "welcomed" from the start into a small portion of the world, not made of soil but of affection, a family.

God himself "chose to come into the world in a human family, which He himself formed. He formed it in a remote village on the outskirts of the Roman Empire. . . . And someone might say: 'But did this

---

4. See John Paul II, Apostolic Exhortation *Familiaris consortio* (November 22, 1981), 66.

God, who comes to save us, waste 30 years there, in that suburban slum?' He wasted 30 years! He wanted this. Jesus' path was in that family."[5]

Knowing they love us

A hundred times a minute there takes place in the world what happened when we were born: "joy that a child is born into the world" (Jn 16:21). True, we are one among many born on the same day . . . Nonetheless we are unique and irreplaceable, and willed from all eternity: "Each of us is the fruit of God's thought. Each of us is willed, each of us is loved, each of us is necessary."[6]

No person enters the world by accident; each is of great value, is worth everything—even someone who perhaps has not known his or her parents, or was adopted by a family. "Each soul is a wonderful treasure; every human being is unique and irreplaceable. Every single person is worth all the blood of Christ."[7]

---

5. Francis, General Audience (December 17, 2014).

6. Benedict XVI, Homily on the Occasion of the Solemn Beginning of the Petrine Ministry of the Bishop of Rome (April 24, 2005).

7. Escrivá, *Christ Is Passing By*, no. 80.

We owe so much to our parents, whoever they may be, despite their weaknesses and difficulties. They know all that God expects of them and strive to respond to his gentle but demanding call: "I was an unborn child, and you welcomed me by letting me be born; I was an abandoned child, and you became my family; I was an orphan, and you adopted me and raised me as one of your own children."[8]

A few weeks after their child's birth, mothers already can distinguish the features of their child's temperament: the tone of their cry, of their sleep, of their hunger. Then comes the first smile: the birth, as it were, of their personality, and at the same time one of the first perceptible signs of the imitation so pronounced in children, who are struck by all that they see. Parents are for a child a source of security, as we often see in the eloquent gesture of a child embracing its mother's or father's legs at the approach of a stranger. From this safe haven, a child learns to move about, to explore the world, and to open up to others.

Although we are not completely determined by the circumstances of birth and upbringing, the harmonious

---

8. John Paul II, Letter to Families *Gratissimam Sane* (February 2, 1994), 22.

development of a child's personality requires that from the first moment that children know they are loved in the family, so they in turn may love others. Affection and attentive care, which includes fostering the fortitude needed to restrain the selfishness to which all are prone, help children to perceive their own value and that of other people. This strong and tender love of their parents gives children the self-esteem that will enable them to love, to get out of themselves.

The bonds of love that arise in a Christian family are not broken even by the end of our lives here on earth. If someone loses their parents in the first years of life, with faith they can see Jesus himself, Our Lady or St. Joseph taking their place, often through other people with a big heart. Following the example of the Holy Family, we strive to be both very human and very supernatural,[9] and keep alive the hope that one day there will happen what St. Teresa related: "It seemed to me that I was taken up to heaven; and the first persons I saw there were my father and my mother."[10]

---

9. Escrivá, *The Forge*, no. 290.

10. Teresa of Avila, *The Life of St. Teresa of Avila*, trans. David Lewis (New York: Cosimo Classics, 2011), 312.

Authentic self-realization

"Mom, did you like cooking? Washing clothes? Cleaning the house? Taking us to school?" These questions by a daughter to her elderly mother reminds the good woman of the times when things didn't turn out well, of the tiredness involved in looking after the home, of financial worries and concern for her young children with a high fever in winter time . . . and even that plate thrown against the wall in a moment of impatience.

"Did I like it? Not really, but I loved you and enjoyed so much seeing you grow up."

How many mothers and fathers behave like this! Many of them should be given a prize, the Pope suggested, because they have learned "to solve an equation that not even the great mathematicians know how to solve: within 24 hours they make twice that many! There are mothers and fathers who could win the Nobel Prize for this! Out of 24 hours they make 48; I don't know how they do it but they get on and do it!"[11]

A family—never perfect, but harmonious—distinguishes clearly the identity of each of its members.

---

11. Francis, General Audience (August 26, 2015).

The parents have authority, but they don't impose it on their children. Their goal is not to "train" their children, but to guide them to develop their full potential with their affectionate example. Both father and mother are responsible for the family environment, and for each of them their dedication to the other spouse and to the children becomes a path for personal growth.

Family life also helps uncover talents that otherwise might have gone unnoticed, but that the others value highly, such as the capacity for affection, fortitude, good humor, and the like. Love for one's family ensures that, even when difficulties arise, each brings out the best in oneself, the positive side of one's temperament. And when, owing to tiredness or tension, the less pleasant side appears, it is the moment to ask for pardon and to begin again. "To acknowledge that we have fallen short, to be desirous of returning what has been taken away—respect, sincerity, love—these make us worthy of pardon. This is how we heal the infection. . . . So many wounds, so many scrapes and bruises are the result of a lack of these precious words: 'I am sorry.'"[12]

In the family, a woman discovers that her qualities as a mother are irreplaceable. The effort to be faithful

---

12. Francis, General Audience (May 13, 2015).

to God in her mission will prompt her to create a welcoming environment that is apt for personal growth, for affection and respect, for sacrifice and self-giving. "Women are called to bring to the family, to society and to the Church, characteristics which are their own and which they alone can give: their gentle warmth and untiring generosity, their love for detail, their quick-wittedness and intuition, their simple and deep piety, their constancy. . . ."[13]

The father also discovers his role as the guide for his children; he helps them grow, plays with them, and lets each one develop their way of being. A Christian father knows that his family will always be his "main business," in which he achieves his true self-fulfillment. Therefore, he needs to be on guard against an overly intense and stressful lifestyle that obscures more valuable goals, and that can even lead to psychological problems and resentment for overlooking family responsibilities.

How important it is, then, that parents be close to their children. Their absence causes so many problems. They need to always foster the pride of passing on to their children their hearts' wisdom.[14] In a "bright and

---

13. Escrivá, *Conversations*, no. 87

14. see Francis, General Audiences (January 28, 2015, and February 4, 2015).

cheerful" home,[15] the father experiences and gives his paternity, and the mother her maternity, complementary and irreplaceable qualities capable of filling the heart. And if God doesn't send them children, they can exercise a spiritual paternity and maternity with other members of their family and with friends.

WAITING AND COMMITMENT

"Perhaps we are not always aware of it, but it is the family that introduces fraternity into the world."[16] The underlying situation of peoples, peace among nations, is grounded on the free self-offering of a man and a woman for love, on their fidelity to a "Yes" that marks their lives forever.

Today the hunger for adventure abounds. The offerings come in many forms, with a great variety of possibilities that are intense, brief, passionate. A definitive commitment is less dramatic, but always awakens admiration, since we are made to love forever and, when all is said and done, everything else seems little to us. A love that was not forever, a "yes" in small letters, would not be love.

---

15. Escrivá, *Christ is Passing By*, no. 78.
16. Francis, General Audience (February 18, 2015).

Family life requires weathering storms and crises, but fidelity to the "Yes" that founded the home can always be stronger than all of these: "love is strong as death" (Song 8:6). Great commitments enable us to bear great difficulties. Here the commitment is not only to an idea or an institution but, above all, to persons. The "Yes" of love enters so deeply into our beings that we cannot deny it without doing great damage to ourselves.

Certainly, every great project involves a great risk, and many young people today are afraid of a "yes" that is forever, because they are afraid of making a mistake. But it is an even greater mistake to remain at the threshold of the love to which our hearts are called. Therefore, a person's heart needs to mature, to grow, so as to love steadily and strongly. This is the Christian meaning of engagement: "a path of life that has to ripen like fruit; it is a way of maturing in love, until the moment it becomes marriage."[17] The best training for this "Yes," the best test of its firmness, is being able to wait. The Church never tires of asking the engaged couple to wait, although at times they may not fully understand the reasons. "Those who claim to want everything right away, then back out of everything—right away—at

---

17. Francis, General Audience (May 27, 2015).

the first difficulty. . . . This is not love! Engagement focuses on the will to care for something together that must never be bought or sold, betrayed or abandoned, however tempting the offer may be."[18]

Children learn a lot from parents who are able to care together for this love. These are the homes that produce the best citizens, prepared to sacrifice themselves for the common good, workers who are honest in what belongs to themselves and to others, enthusiastic teachers, noble politicians, just lawyers, self-sacrificing doctors, and so on. In the warmth of these homes new mothers and fathers grow up who will be faithful, and many young people who will dedicate themselves completely to God, in order to serve the human family in a vocation where maternity or paternity also shines forth.

With the passage of time the adventure continues. The walls become too small, new homes and new loves spring up. Enthusiasm and the joy of living are reborn. Therefore "[t]here is a close link between the hope of a people and the harmony among generations. The joy of children causes the parents' hearts to beat and reopens the future."[19]

---

18. Francis.

19. Francis, General Audience (February 11, 2015).

9

Details of the Home

Wenceslao Vial

THE FAMILY IS THE SCHOOL OF GRATUITOUS
AND SINCERE LOVE.

The fire crackles in the fireplace during a heated conversation about a battle dating from ancient times.
One of Dickens characters, in his Christmas story
"The Battle of Life," then makes a surprising declara-
tion: "I believe there are quiet victories and struggles,
great sacrifices of self, and noble acts of heroism in it
(even in many of its apparently lighter moments and
contradictions) not the less difficult to achieve, because
they have no earthly chronicle or audience, done every
day in nooks and crannies, in little households, and
in men's and women's hearts. Any one of these might

reconcile the sternest man with the world, and fill him
with belief and hope in it."[1]

The world's future is forged not only in major
international decisions, however crucial they might
seem. It is decided especially in small daily struggles,
the "patient love"[2] that is the discreet work of grandparents, parents and children. The project of growth,
a growth that is above all "on the inside,"[3] lasts a whole
lifetime for each person, and is necessarily a matter of
teamwork, all moving "at God's pace," spurred forward
by his breath in the sails of our souls.

Breathing the same air

In a family with a Christian atmosphere, jobs, concerns, successes and failures are all shared. Everything belongs to everybody, while each one's personal
interests are also respected. Children are taught to be
themselves, but to avoid isolating themselves in their
own tastes and preferences. Cell phones, the social

1. Charles Dickens, "The Battle of Life," in *The Christmas Books*,
vol. 1 (London: Penguin, 1972), p. 245.

2. Francis, *Homily for The Family Day on the Occasion of the Year
of Faith* (October 27, 2013).

3. Escrivá, *The Way*, no. 294.

networks, the Internet can all find a natural place in the home, without controlling life there and stifling conversations and interest in one another. Everyone needs to know how to "disconnect" in order to connect with others in real life. Entertaining moments are spent together, with conversations at meals that are continued afterwards, in which both young and old take part. Importance is given at home to whatever can unite, like fresh air allowing each one to breathe freely, to fill their lungs and develop.

In this effort to strengthen the family atmosphere, everyone is important, even the youngest. It is good to give children little responsibilities, in keeping with their age. Thus they are helped to get out of themselves and discover that the smooth functioning of the home requires everyone working together: for instance, watering a plant, setting the table, making one's bed and tidying one's room, taking care of a younger sibling, or going shopping. Little by little, they are allowed to share in making decisions; family plans are not simply imposed, but presented in an attractive way. Thus no one is left out, and children are helped to be open, generous, and concerned about the world and other people.

Affection leads to living united, to sharing with others the new episodes of each one's own life story. It can be helpful to share times of rest and recreation in common, with activities that unite and allow the enjoyment of so many good things. Then when sorrow or misfortune arise, charity leads us to want to share the weight: "Bear one another's burdens, and so fulfil the law of Christ" (Gal 6:2). No one can live as a stranger in one's own house. Each one needs to have initiative, and open his or her eyes and pay attention to the others, to their hobbies, plans, friendship, work, and concerns. Certainly this requires time, which is truly the best gift that parents can give their children, and that children can give their parents.

A Christian family also needs discipline—but present in a pleasant way. Then children find learning enjoyable and grow step by step with the example of older siblings. Correction is accompanied by good manners and affection. The "whys and wherefores" are explained, while trying "to keep our bad humor or temper to ourselves."[4] Sometimes one needs to be particularly clear, but good parents never forget that virtues and values take root effectively when children see them embodied in the lives of their own parents. Fortitude, temperance, decorum and modesty, shown

---

4. Escrivá, *Christ Is Passing By*, no. 174.

in daily life, are then seen by them as genuine goods that become a natural part of their life, like the air they breathe. This applies particularly to the guidance of their emotions and feelings. Parents who outwardly express their mutual affection in the small points of daily life, although without displays of affection that should be kept within the intimacy of the spouses, introduce their children into the mystery of true love between a man and a woman.

"If I were to give advice to parents, I would tell them, above all, let your children see that you are trying to live in accordance with your faith. Don't let yourself be deceived: they see everything. Let them see that God is not only on your lips, but also in your deeds. Let them see that you are trying to be loyal and sincere, and that you love each other and you really love them too."[5]

Thank You; Please; I'm Sorry

In a "bright and cheerful home,"[6] people treat one another in a simple and trusting way. Good manners are practiced at all times and not just reserved for

---

5. Escrivá, no. 28.

6. Escrivá, no. 78.

visitors, with small details that make life pleasant for others. The husband tries to dress well, and the wife to care for her appearance even after the years go by; good taste in household decorations, a special dessert for an important occasion, all help make the affection in the home visible and provide a healthy atmosphere for growing.

Care also needs to be taken to ensure that this closeness does not give way to insensitivity or insolence. We all have defects. We can make a mistake and wound others, but we have the capacity to overlook misunderstandings, and not harbor resentment. At every level, from parents to children, from children to parents, or among siblings, we have to focus on the positive, on what unites.

Wherever people live with one another, at times arguments or quarrels arise. But it's worthwhile making the effort to end each day reconciled with the others. It's the moment to put into practice Christ's teaching on not putting limits to forgiveness (cf. Mt 18:21–22). Besides, asking for forgiveness matures one's own soul and the soul of the one who receives or witnesses a sincere expression of regret. "Listen to me carefully: did you fight with your wife or husband? Kids—did you fight with your parents? Did you seriously argue? That's not a good thing, but it's not really that which is the problem: the problem arises only if this feeling hangs over into the next day. So if you've fought, do not let the day end without making peace with your family."[7]

Whoever really wants to, is able and even needs to understand and excuse others. And this good atmosphere is exported from the family to the world. To transform the jungle, we need to start with our own gardens, with an "ecology of daily life," given expression "in our rooms, our homes, our workplaces and neighborhoods."[8] The family is the place where we "receive an integral education, which enables us to grow harmoniously in personal maturity. In the family we learn to ask without demanding, to say 'thank you' as an expression of genuine gratitude for what we have been given, to control our aggressivity and greed, and to ask forgiveness when we have caused harm."[9]

This attitude helps us to place in perspective problems that can arise in our lives alongside others, and to reject the thought that in other circumstances

---

7. Francis, General Audience (May 13, 2015).

8. Francis, *Laudato si'*, 147; cf. General Audience (May 13, 2015).

9. Francis, *Laudato si'*, 213.

everything would be simpler. It is usually easier to judge more positively those who do not actually live with us. Even psychologically well-balanced people tend to idealize what is good in their friends and acquaintances, while highlighting the defects and errors of their closer family members. But we need to confront and overcome these prejudices! The smiling and friendly demeanor of those we seldom see doesn't always reflect the way things really are. Nor does the brusque remark of a brother or sister, after a bad day or night, reflect their whole personality, or the real view they have of us. Moreover, it is good to realize that, when we have greater confidence with someone, it is only natural that they lower their guard a bit and give vent to what is weighing on them, in one way or another. Part of real affection then means trying to be understanding, and providing a shoulder to cry on, if needed.

The stages of development, with their respective crises, are challenges that require patience, because maturity is rarely achieved in one go. The atmosphere in a home is especially affected by adolescence, more or less prolonged, which can sometimes result in disagreements and nervousness in both adults and children. But as time goes by, if the crisis has been well addressed, the family comes out strengthened. Not only do the waters return to their proper channels, but they become stronger and healthier.

It is normal that children, when they reach adolescence, need more scope for their freedom, to form their own circle of friends and learn to fend for themselves. Parents will continue being their frame of reference, but their youthful vitality will make it hard for them to accept it. Therefore parents need to be more than simply the "authority" at home; they also need to foster a friendly and trust-filled relationship with their children. Parents should encourage their children to make their own decisions, while also pointing out possible pitfalls. They should show them both the "reefs" they may encounter in making their way in life as well as the "beacon" that can guide them safely. And this wisdom is passed on more by example than by many words or rules, although naturally some may be necessary.

In any case, children should be trusted, because freedom flourishes only in a climate of trust. As St. Josemaría used to say, it is even better that parents "let themselves be fooled once in a while, because the trust that they have shown will make children themselves feel ashamed for having abused it. They will then correct themselves. On the other hand, if they see that no one trusts them, they will always be inclined to deceive their parents."[10]

A FAMILY THAT PRAYS TOGETHER STAYS TOGETHER

In the family, children also learn how to turn to God, to pray. How much St. Josemaría appreciated the prayers his mother taught him! "Without mothers, not only would there be no new faithful, but the faith would lose a good deal of its simple and profound warmth."[11] Normally it is the parents who teach their children how to draw close to God; but not infrequently their roles are reversed, and Providence makes use of the children to teach a father or mother the marvelous "melody" of the faith.

Often ways will be found to pray together, mindful of the adage, "the family that prays together, stays together."[12] A piety that is transparent and sincere sheds light within and outside the home, in serene harmony with other daily occupations. It doesn't

---

10. Escrivá, *Conversations*, no. 100.

11. Pope Francis, *Audience*, 7 January 2015.

12. John Paul II, Apostolic Letter *Rosarium Virginis Mariae*, 41.

matter if distractions sometimes arise, with children coming and going and many tasks at home that need to be covered. When we do what we can, these distractions are not discordant notes but rather harmonious music in heaven.

Faithful parents beget new faithful parents, and also many young people who, accepting God's invitation, follow a vocational path in celibacy. Neither love for another human being nor love for God are in competition with affection for our own families, but rather increase it. At every moment of life, the same blood always runs through our veins. We are united, even when separated by great distances and new commitments and obligations. One sign of maturity is precisely the ability, learned over time, to combine the duties arising from the new home we form with an ever stronger filial and fraternal affection for the family we were born in. We count on their prayers for our mission in life, and we support them with our own. For "a brother helped is like a strong city" (Prv 18:19).

FROM THE HOME TO THE PERIPHERY

The great potential of a family is not meant to be closed up within itself. Just as it would be impossible to mature if one were centered on oneself, so family life grows by opening itself to the world outside. A Christian home certainly needs doors to protect its intimacy, to provide the right environment for growth, but these can't be closed so tightly that they suffocate or block the vision of those inside.

Solidarity, therefore, is an important part of the mission of Christian families. This requires going out creatively to help the neediest, trying to help all men and women attain the culture and education they need, caring for the earth as our common home. The needs of those around us are quite varied and often do not align with the priorities that some ideologies and small groups strive to impose upon the world. What great examples we have in families that seek to assist homeless immigrants; large families that welcome a new child; parents who sacrifice themselves for their own children and for those of others, overcoming financial problems heroically; childless couples who devote their lives to helping other families.

And the best thing about all this effort is that everything starts within the home. The first who stand to gain from these initiatives are one's own family members. And from the home one reaches the whole world. The family, a school of gratuitous and sincere love, is "the strongest antidote to the spread of self-centered individualism."[13] Those who have grown up with "the 'healthy psychological prejudice' of usually thinking about others,"[14] enjoy listening to, learning to understand, getting along with and solving the specific needs of their fellow men and women.

FAMILIES NOT ALONE

The big picture for families, their role in the Church and the world, is an exciting one. At the same time, the difficulties they face are evident to all. But families are not alone. Many good people spend time and energy helping parents in their educative task. Schools, youth clubs and many other initiatives can be a decisive support in the effort to care for young people, and also for the elderly.

Striving to assist and facilitate domestic work, a task that is not exclusive to mothers, is another pillar of Christian homes. Therefore St. Josemaría once told those who dedicate their lives to passing on to others their knowledge and experience in this field that they

---

13. Francis, General Audience (January 7, 2015).

14. Escrivá, *The Forge*, no. 861.

are "more effective educators then many university professors."[15] Sharing the work at home, with a list of jobs, is important in order to ensure everyone gets enough rest and has time for family conversations and outings together with the others.

Finally, what can we tell those who, despite all their diligent efforts, think they should have done more? Many parents who have done all they could to raise their children well, have then seen them undergo material and spiritual problems, and fail to practice their faith or fall into disordered lives. Besides deepening their own formation in order to foresee and prevent problems, if difficult situations do arise then is the time to have greater recourse to heaven, perhaps saying: *My God, now it's your turn to act. Take care of them and protect them, since they are your children too and you have suffered for them.* Unwavering and trusting prayer can transform apparent defeats, as St. Monica saw so clearly after asking insistently for the conversion of her son Augustine.

Like the father in the Gospel parable who, without forcing his son's freedom, goes out to meet him,

---

15. Escrivá, *Conversations*, no. 88.

parents have to always be ready to assist any of their children who have distanced themselves, at the smallest sign of the desire to correct their ways (cf. Lk 15:20). Renewed affection—shown in small details of understanding, staying close and asking for forgiveness if necessary, and other family reminders—can be the light that draws the disoriented one back home. Parents "must be patient. Often there is nothing else to do but wait; pray and wait with patience, gentleness, magnanimity and mercy."[16]

16. Francis, General Audience (February 4, 2015).

10

The Others and I: Verses of the Same Poem

Carlos Ayxelá

WE NEED OTHERS, AND THEY NEED US.

"And God saw that it was good" (cf. Gen 1:10, 12, 18, 21, 25).[1] Against the background of this refrain that resonates throughout the entire first account of the creation of the world, we are presented with the contrast of the second account. In this second narrative "the Holy Spirit evokes God's thoughts, even His emotion, as He gazes at Adam, observing him alone in the garden. He is free, he is a lord . . . but he is alone.

---

1. Verse 31 adds, "And God saw everything that he had made, and behold, it was very good."

And God sees that this 'is not good.'"[2] The loneliness of man is like a piece that fails to fit into the design of creation. When God finally presents Eve to Adam, as bone of his bones and flesh of his flesh (cf. Gen 2:23), Adam is freed from a strange melancholy that he himself cannot explain. Now he is truly able to say with God that "everything is good." Strengthened in his vocation upon meeting *others like himself*, the world ceases to be for him an inhospitable place.

Living alongside others develops our personalities, but the reality is much richer than this. We need others, and they need us. They are never superfluous; they are the "land" to which we always belong and from which God calls us to receive and welcome everyone. Because we have a history, a family, a neighborhood, a culture, each of us is a "home," a place of welcome, and can create a home wherever we go. Because we have a home, we can view the world as a home, as our own home and, at the same time, as "our common home."[3] Affection for our roots, the serene cultivation of our ways of being, enables us to love and to be loved, to welcome and to be welcomed.

---

2. Francis, Audience (April 22, 2015); cf. *Gen* 2:18.

3. Francis, *Laudato Si'*, 13.

WITH OTHERS AND FOR OTHERS

One of the key experiences in our lives is the concern others have shown us. Someone has cared for us, has raised us. Each of us has been "received" by others. No one grows up alone. And no one is really alone, even though some people's lives seem to develop this way. The breakdown of the family and the resulting abandonment in which many children live, does not make this basic anthropological principle a beautiful but useless idea. Not a few people who have grown up in a hostile environment and been damaged by a lack of love, are for that very reason especially sensitive to the need for affection. They can become a welcoming "haven" for others. Whoever has suffered much can love much.

"No human life is ever isolated. It is bound up with other lives. No man or woman is a single verse; we all make up one divine poem which God writes with the cooperation of our freedom."[4] Others are not simply objects near us, like a stone by the side of the road. They belong to us and we belong to them, more intimately than we can imagine. We will understand this fully in heaven, although on earth we can catch

---

4. Escrivá, *Christ Is Passing by*, no. 111.

a glimpse of it, in striving to live close to God and to those around us. This mutual belonging to one another has two very important implications: others depend on me, and I can and should depend on them.

To love and to let oneself be loved: the path to maturity that is always open to us passes through incorporating into our own lives these two aspects of our being "with others and for others."[5]

Widening the "I"

Adolescence is the first moment when this challenge comes clearly to the fore. Up to this time the parents have formed the heart of the person who now begins to walk on his or her own. Although everything has a remedy, this previous work by parents determines in good measure how young people look on the world and what captures their attention.

Adolescents readily tend to choose role models different from their own parents, as they begin to sense the need to assert themselves. Their feelings here tend to be somewhat ambivalent. Alongside the perception of their dependence on their parents, they sense a thirst

5. Francis, *Evangelii Gaudium*, 273.

for emancipation, and therefore love for their parents goes hand in hand with a certain rejection of their own home. They are just starting out in life, but want to be convinced that their situation is secure. They want to be different, but also to belong to a group. It's a difficult moment for young people and also for parents. But underlying these at times exaggerated attempts to assert themselves lies the need to broaden their own self-identities.

Infancy is marked by the tendency to refer everything to one's own "I" or "ego." With the gradual arrival of maturity, the "I" expands and opens up to others. One begins to perceive that others have needs, and to feel the personal responsibility to help them. *Others exist*, each with his or her own concerns and aspirations. A clear sign of immaturity is precisely the inability to confront this new demand in life.

Over-protective parents, a badly understood affection, an excessive zeal to protect their child from life's difficulties and challenges, can lead to this personality defect. Later on, when the child grows up, this can result in negligent fathers or mothers who live for their own work and interests, and who fail to take an interest in the upbringing of their own children; in property owners who show no interest in their neighborhood community, and who always seem to be in conflict with those around them; in unhappy persons who accumulate grievances in order to convince themselves that conflicts are always due to others.

GIFTS ARE FOR SERVING OTHERS

We belong to others. This conviction, purified of servility or naiveté, is a clear sign of maturity. It means that in a certain sense *my time is not my own*, because the others need me. Rest, entertainment, cultural and professional formation then acquire a broader perspective. The border between what is mine and what belongs to others becomes less sharp, without neglecting our own responsibilities or infringing on others' freedom. This is how a Christian should always view the world. "If the Lord has given you some natural quality or skill, you should not just enjoy it yourself or show off about it; you should use it charitably in the service of your neighbor."[6]

Egotism disconnects us from reality. It makes us forget that everything in our lives is a gift. "What have you that you did not receive? If then you received it,

---

6. Escrivá, *Furrow*, 422.

why do you boast as if it were not a gift?" (1 Cor 4:7).
If everything we have is a gift, even more so are other
people. Nevertheless at times we live as if they didn't
exist, or we submit them in subtle ways to our own
judgment or interests. Rather than receiving them, we
appropriate them.

"Each person tends to install himself in a very
comfortable corner, and the others can fend for themselves."[7] The tendency to make the world revolve
around our own egos is a sign of immaturity that we
have to strive to overcome bit by bit, serenely. We will
then come to see our lives not in the light of our own
private successes, but as a contribution to everyone's
happiness. Thus we will discover, and re-discover, that
true fulfillment is never just *self-fulfillment*. "We do not
live better when we flee, hide, refuse to share, stop giving and lock ourselves up in our own comforts. Such a
life is nothing less than slow suicide. . . . I am a mission on this earth; that is the reason why I am here in
this world. We have to regard ourselves as sealed, even
branded, by this mission of bringing light, blessing,
enlivening, raising up, healing and freeing."[8]

---

7. Josemaría Escrivá, as quoted in notes taken at a family gathering on October 21, 1973.

8. Francis, *Evangelii Gaudium*, 272–273.

In any group of people, those who want to help
others can always find ample space for doing so. Daily
life constantly presents new and unforeseen challenges. Families and societies go forward thanks to
these gratuitous efforts. These generous people, perhaps surrounded by the apathy of those who prefer
not to complicate their lives, realize how much they
owe to others for their bodily and spiritual growth.
They know that they are called to the same self-giving that truly liberates a person: fathers and mothers
who raise families, children who help their parents,
students who help their fellow students, workers who
confront problems that others avoid. "When you have
finished your work, do your brother's, helping him,
for Christ, so tactfully and naturally that no one—
not even he—will realize you are doing more than in
justice you ought. This, indeed, is virtue befitting a
son of God."[9]

This generosity is clearly far removed from the "servility" of those who undertake all sorts of tasks, without helping others to be demanding on themselves, as
well as from the naiveté of those who let others take
advantage of their good intentions. Serving does not

---

9. Escrivá, *The Way*, no. 440.

always mean doing things. It implies above all helping others to grow, and this also leads to leaving space for each one's personal responsibility.

BEING CLOSE TO OTHERS

Today's world tends to seek technical solutions for almost every problem, and overlooks at times the human warmth provided by mutual help. Nevertheless, when faced with situations that shake our sense of security, for example, a natural disaster or major accident, solidarity spontaneously surfaces, a sense of community often hidden under the demands of daily life. Once again things that unite people come to the fore, as though awakening from an enchantment. People focus once again on what is essential. The same happens on a smaller scale in personal misfortunes like the death or illness of a loved one; or in daily interactions that for various reasons suddenly affect us more deeply: for instance, when someone makes us realize, even in a subtle way, the "bitterness of indifference,"[10] the coldness that freezes the soul. Or on the contrary, when we sense the warmth of a sincere interest in

---

10. Josemaría Escrivá, Letter (March 11, 1940), no. 7.

ourselves, then the soul awakens to what is really important, the need to welcome others.

"I was a stranger and you welcomed me" (Mt 25:35). We all are in some way strangers and pilgrims, and we hope that others will welcome us: that they will comfort us, that they will listen to us, that they will look us in the eye. Maturity means acquiring this sensitivity towards others, and sometimes requires overlooking another person's lack of sensitivity for other people, even though this makes us suffer. At times it could be appropriate to advise people who err in this way, and help them see their lack of tact. At other times, the best strategy could be the "contagion" of our own example; refined example sooner or later awakens the sensitivity of even the roughest of people.

This sensitivity also leads people to undertake initiatives that make an impact on the immediate surroundings. For example, "show concern for a public place (a building, a fountain, an abandoned monument, a landscape, a square), and strive to protect, restore, improve or beautify it as something belonging to everyone. Around these community actions, relationships develop or are recovered and a new social fabric emerges. Thus, a community can break out of the indifference induced by consumerism. . . . In this way, the world, and the quality of life of the poorest, are cared for, with a sense of solidarity which is at the same time aware that we live in a common home which God has entrusted to us."[11]

The maturity that this closeness to others entails is not the same as the facility for relationships found in loquacious or extroverted persons. It is a matter above all of knowing how to *be present* with others: to observe, listen, welcome, to learn from everyone. Especially nowadays, when communication technology allows us to relate to many people, rediscovering the meaning of a genuine personal *presence* with others is all the more necessary. A smartphone allows us to contact someone immediately, but doesn't bring us closer to them.

In the virtual world, we can decide who are our "neighbors" and "friends." And paradoxically this can make us lose sight of the people life has placed alongside us. Even though a common sight today, it is still disturbing to see a group of people together who, instead of talking with one another, are "managing" their respective text messages. Virtual communication then absorbs real communication. Almost without realizing it, our lives becomes focused on seeing if

11. Francis, *Laudato si'*, 232.

someone has remembered us, instead of realizing that *this person alongside me needs me!* And the best thing I can give that person is my closeness to them.

Opting for this personal presence, in which we open ourselves to direct contact with others, to reality without filters, strengthens our humanity. It awakens us once again to what is truly important. Thinking about others, praying for them, leads us to live for them. "This is the only way to live the life of Jesus Christ and to become one and the same with Him."[12]

---

12. Escrivá, *The Way of the Cross*, XIV.

11

The Ripe Fruit
of Personal Identity

Wenceslao Vialé

A PERSON'S IDENTITY IS LIKE A DIAMOND THAT IS
SHAPED SLOWLY UNTIL IT BECOMES A JEWEL.

Who am I? When we go for a job interview, when
we go through customs at the airport, when we try
to access an article on the Internet, and on many
other occasions, we are asked to give personal data. It
is easy to provide such information as name, date of
birth, occupation, nationality, height, weight and the
color of our eyes. . . . We may even list certain features of our character: whether we are good at sports;
whether we tend to put on weight easily; whether we
are optimistic or pessimistic, extroverted or shy. But

isn't it true that, in the end, we still haven't answered the question *who am I?*

At the beginning of these pages we saw that a mature Christian has a clear and sublime goal in life, illuminated by one's vocation as a child of God. Being aware of this goal and making it our own is what helps us to better define ourselves. Successive chapters have helped us understand personal growth and signs of maturity, which includes the action of the Holy Spirit in our soul. From the start of this process and right through to its end, our identity is always a work in progress, like a diamond that is shaped slowly until it shines and takes on great value.

As young children we already know who we are, and we begin to glimpse the goal, even when everything is yet to be achieved. Little by little, our identities strengthen and we become more aware of our value and mission in the world; we recognize our limitations and talents; we discover the good and evil existing in others.

At the outset, our parents make the decisions for us. They choose our names and what we are to eat; they give us the faith, and select a school for us . . . As we enter adolescence, our distinctive characteristics become more apparent, and we spread our wings for an autonomous, though never solitary, flight. By the end of our earthly existence, a life filled with meaning comes to a close with a well-defined identity. Thus the story of our lives that we have tried to write with God's hand guiding our pen-strokes will come to an end, and there will open up before us our true stories: we will find again, along with the "hundredfold" (Mt 19:29), all we have loved, and all the people *with whom* we have loved.

AIMING AT THE BULLSEYE

Like the archer shooting an arrow, if we want to hit the target we have to aim high. We have to keep our ideals in view and head steadily towards them. A mature person tries to refocus on the goal before starting a new task, or before making a decision, so as not to mistake the means for the end. By knowing who we are and where we are going, we will not be deceived by the appearance of happiness promised by easy pleasures, or by the illusion of autonomy enjoyed by those who accept only their own viewpoint. To take sure aim at the target, we need to rely on the experience of someone who tells us how taut the bowstring should be, how to hold the bow, and how to pay attention to what is really important. An onlooker may try to help us by telling us where our shots are ending up and correct us in a friendly and assured manner: higher, more to the right, more to the left, make allowances for the wind, and so on. This is what parents try to do, or good educators or friends, or a priest who gives us advice on the Christian life.

Being docile to the suggestions of those who love us and to the promptings of God in our souls is the key for reaching the desired goal. To hit the target we have to aim right at the bullseye, but we can get distracted and look in other directions, ignoring all signs and warnings. It is not enough, therefore, to know the goal; we need to strive to pursue it at every moment, to persevere and ask for help.

So often we find it hard to change, to alter our ways of being. Nevertheless, our responses to these limitations can vary greatly and significantly influences our joy and the ability to share it with others. The way we act and react marks our personalities. *In omnibus respice finem*, as an ancient heraldic motto says: *In everything you do, keep your gaze fixed upon your end*. At work or at rest, asleep or awake, we are always the same, with the same identity that never vanishes: an identity that it would make no sense to hide. Being afraid to show ourselves as we are is a clear symptom of a weak and wavering identity. Christians see God as their Father, and are concerned not so much about what to expect from life, as about what God and life expect from them.[1]

If we often ask ourselves what God wants from us and try to please him, we become stronger and more consistent men and women. We not only know who we are, but also how to act in every situation. Our identities mature in our occupations and take shape with our personal characteristics. We are happy to be ourselves and to do what we do. A filial and trusting spirit marks our relationships with God, even when we fail to understand something or we experience personal weakness. Each Christian "identity card" is the same as that of Jesus, and also has his Cross as its distinctive sign.[2] By getting to know Christ we get to know ourselves better. By looking steadily at Christ, and with his powerful help, we will hit the bullseye.

---

1. Cf. Victor Frankl, *Man's Search for Meaning*.

2. Cf. Francis. Morning Meditation in the Chapel of the Domus Sanctae Marthae (September 26, 2014), as quoted in "True Identity." *L'Osservatore Romano*, Weekly ed. in English, n. 40 (October 3, 2014).

The "Our Father," a sure guide

Jesus, through his life and teachings, is our model. We receive from him the name of Christian and our own prayer, the Our Father (cf. Mt 6:9–13), which provides an excellent guide for each human life and character. This prayer teaches us what we ought to seek, and the order in which we ought to ask for it. Our experiences, our readings, the images captured by our retinas, spur us forward or hold us back. So many factors help us to advance or cause us to veer off the track. Prayer guides us in the midst of all this complexity, as we try to write a new page each day in our life stories.

We have prayed the Our Father so often, but we can always be dazzled by it again. We realize once again that our Father God in heaven is watching over us: not outside or far away, but very close to us.[3] We don't say *my* but *our* Father, because being human means being in relation to others. We ask that his *name* be *hallowed*. He doesn't need anything, and yet he wants to be known, adored, sought, and glorified, because only then can mankind satisfy its hunger for happiness.[4]

---

3. Cf. Escrivá, *The Way*, no. 267.

4. Cf. Benedict XVI, Homily during the Pastoral Visit to Ancona (11 September 2011).

And we go on to request: *Thy Kingdom come.* Our
personal lives are illumined by this aspiration, which is
made true in Christ, by his grace acting in us, leading
us to eternal glory. "This Christian identity, as the bap-
tismal embrace which the Father gave us when we were
little ones, makes us desire, as prodigal children, and
favorite children in Mary, yet another embrace, that of
the merciful Father who awaits us in glory."[5]

Thy Will be done on earth as it is in heaven: help
our lives to be oriented toward you, foundation and
goal of our personal identity. All our successes and
failures, joys and sorrows, are then viewed from this
perspective.

We recognize ourselves as creatures in need of
material goods, of *our daily bread.* Besides, on a deeper
level, this bread refers to the Eucharist, to Jesus himself, who invites us to receive him. During the Mass, at
the end of the Eucharistic Prayer, the priest addresses
the congregation saying: ". . . *we dare to say,*" and then
he joins the people in reciting the prayer that our Lord
taught us. *Daily:* today and now is the time to choose
him, to amend our lives in accord with God's will, to
forgive and not to hold grudges.

---

5. Francis, *Evangelii Gaudium*, 144.

Once, in a country where believers were a minority, during a class on the local language for foreigners, the teacher asked a Christian student: "What does God do?" as she pointed to the word *punish* in the dictionary. That student found himself in a quandary because even though he thought that the teacher's statement was unfair, he didn't feel confident enough to give a full explanation. Nevertheless, he surprised his classmates by simply saying, "God forgives." We ask God to help us share in that feature so characteristic of him, by which we come to resemble him. How can we fail to hear Jesus' words as addressed to each one of us: "forgive us our trespasses, as we forgive those who trespass against us"?[6]

We end by saying, "lead us not into temptation, but deliver us from evil." We want God to fill us with his love, with his mercy, which not only involves forgiving but also alerts us to dangers along the way. Through his Church, God points out to us what we should avoid. The Beatitudes in the Sermon on the Mount set forth a demanding program that leads to a virtuous and peaceful life. In contrast, sin not only

---

6. *The Roman Missal, English Translation according to the Third Typical Edition* (New York: Magnificat, 2011), 647.

offends God, but it also harms us and robs us of our serenity, because it divides our hearts, and "[n]o one can serve two masters" (Mt 6:24). Therefore we are grateful on being told where it is safe to place our feet when climbing, and where to place our hopes in order to see them fulfilled. Through prayer, our identities set down deep roots. We discover that our lives are a constant dialogue with God. And "[i]f God is for us, who is against us?" (Rom 8:31).

STAKING EVERYTHING ON ONE BET

With our eyes raised on high, we direct our steps towards heaven. We know that "Christ has asked us for all our love, all our life, all our heart, all our mind. And we need to respond by staking everything on one bet, God's love. Lord, I love you simply because I want to."[7] Our Christian identities are forged by responding to God's gifts and demands, as we follow our vocations. Each of our actions, our interpersonal relationships with our friends and our colleagues at work, should carry this seal. Our identities require being consistent with the call God has addressed to us.

---

7. Josemaría Escrivá as quoted in notes taken at a family gathering on November 30, 1960..

Maturity is a task that never ends, and therefore giving consistency to our lives means learning to be who we really are. Whoever wants to win a game or a bet usually takes many factors into account and doesn't risk too much. But on the Christian path, we abandon everything into God's hands. Our whole lives acquire meaning from this goal. Love for God, which is impossible without a real love for others shown in deeds, unifies our way of being. When we discover a clear mission in life that fulfills us, we thank the one who helped us to see it, and we put our trust in him. A well-defined Christian identity leads to risking everything on God once and for all. That is the "risky security of the Christian."[8]

The goal of our Christian vocation is identification with Christ. If we are consistent, if we live with naturalness and simplicity, we will recognize Him, since He praises those in whom "there is no guile" (Jn 1:47). In contrast, "all that is tangled and complicated, the twisting and turning about one's own problems, all this builds up a barrier which often prevents people from hearing our Lord's voice."[9] Developing our identities

---

8. Escrivá, *Christ Is Passing By*, no. 58.

9. St. Josemaría, *Friends of God*, no. 90.

means getting rid of the barriers that seem to provide a false security; we have to remove the walls that separate us from others and from God. In Jesus, earth and heaven are united. Identifying ourselves with him means finding out the truths about ourselves.

A SUPERNATURAL IDENTITY

Only the human person is capable of actions that become eloquent gestures, and a language filled with meaning. In the human person, the body's beauty shines forth, a beauty that is protected by modesty, a sign of identity and a space for freedom. Only in mankind can instincts become tendencies, since we can know the purpose of our impulses and learn to control them. We are not meant to be dragged along by blind forces, but to govern them with our intellect and will. Only man and woman were created by God in his image and likeness, as persons (cf. *Gen* 1:26). He destined them to receive education and mature little by little. He destined them, above all, to participate in his intimacy, to build on human foundations a supernatural identity.

This identity does not isolate us but is formed with others and for others. It leads us to forget about ourselves and to look outward. We see this in a baby who, after a few months, begins to recognize his mother's face and smiles. Later on he discovers that he is not the "master" of the world; he stops claiming everything as his own and stops saying "Mine! Mine!" A teenager learns that he cannot demand everything. If he wants his parents to buy him a bicycle, he waits before asking, and perhaps will try to improve his behavior until his birthday arrives. Thus he learns the value of waiting, which prepares him for the true waiting, filled with optimism: Christian hope. As we grow up and mature, we begin to realize that freedom means not only the capacity to choose, but also responsibility: something or someone expects a response from us.

Therefore forming our own personality is not first of all a question of our own fulfillment, but rather of developing our openness to others and improving whatever we can do for them. This task begins in the home, in the family. "[A] family marked by loving trust, come what may, helps its members to be themselves and spontaneously to reject deceit, falsehood, and lies."[10] In a family, each one learns who he or she is and what can be done for others.

------

10. Francis, *Amoris laetitia*, 115.

Astonishment at such a wonderful divine plan leads to the question about the meaning of our existence: *Who am I?* Our fragile identity as creatures rests on the full identity that only God possesses. Our first brothers and sisters in the faith understood it well: "Christians live in the flesh, but not according to the flesh. They spend their lives on earth, but are citizens of heaven."[11]

---

11. *Letter to Diognetus*, 5. (PG 2, 1174).

Epilogue

We have considered in the pages above some of the signs of maturity, by which we build up our life brick by brick. Psychological concepts have gone hand in hand with the virtues, which ennoble our being because they draw out what is best in our humanity. Like a pyramid, the apex of Christian maturity rises high above the broad and strong foundation of faith. Our faith tells us that we are creatures, and that an all-knowing and loving God has given us a mission in life. He offers us the best human identity possible, and fills us with a joy that has no merely human explanation.

"How lucky you are to believe in God," a friend told me. Certainly, many people without faith strive to be faithful and loyal to their family and work commitments. They too are on the path to maturity, because they act with responsibility. The characteristics of a mature personality can be found in any person, and are not in any essential way distinct from those proper to Christian maturity. Christians however enjoy a distinct advantage. They aren't limited to looking at themselves in a mirror, in introspection, to try to find their true meaning. A Christian "sees" himself or herself in Christ, and aspires "to become more and more like Him, the only and most lovable Model."[1] Christians know that theirs is not a solitary effort, since it means above all letting the Holy Spirit model the image of Christ in them. In Jesus they find the firm rock on which to build and the key for deciphering the dilemmas in their life, including suffering.

At the end of their life, Christians aspire to exclaim, in harmony with their traveling companions and those they encountered on the roadside: "there is laid up for me the crown of righteousness, which the Lord, the righteous judge, will award to me on that Day, and not only to me but also to all who have loved his appearing" (2 Tim 4:7–8). Without faith in a future that will last forever, it is much easier to let oneself be led by apparent good, by sparks of pleasure, and fall into resentment or despair.

In constructing this "pyramid," on top of the solid foundation of faith there rises the central block of hope, indispensable for acting with autonomy. Only

---

1. Escrivá, *The Forge*, no. 752.

the confidence that we can finish a task spurs us to seek the means we need and to begin working. A person with hope launches out to conquer the time that lies ahead, without remaining trapped in the past, in "a faint melancholy, lacking in hope, which seizes the heart."[2] With hope we can rise above whatever happens in our lives, and confront events more calmly and with good humor, overcoming setbacks. If something turns out badly, we can begin again and draw good out of "disasters." The story is told that the chef for the Austrian emperor, thinking he had produced a masterpiece of a dessert, drew out of the oven a crumpled and fractured blob. Without becoming discouraged, he used his ingenuity and served it mixed with a delicious fruit sauce. The result received such high praise that even today it is known as the "Kaiserschmarren," the "Emperor's Mess."

Those who live facing God and hoping in him don't give importance to what others might say. If they do something wrong, they acknowledge their guilt and ask for forgiveness. Their shame is turned into repentance (if necessary, with confession, the sacrament of mercy) and they begin again. They are capable of making

---

2. Francis, *Evangelii Gaudium*, 83.

definitive decisions in life, including giving themselves in matrimony or celibacy, and use the means needed to be faithful in moments of trial. They know there is someone they can turn to, the Holy One who loves them and asks for their response. Christians are not engaged in a solitary endeavor, with a totally selfish autonomy. "[W]e want to enter fully into the fabric of society, sharing the lives of all, listening to their concerns, helping them materially and spiritually in their needs, rejoicing with those who rejoice, weeping with those who weep; arm in arm with others, we are committed to building a new world."[3]

At the peak of the "pyramid" we find charity. Love for God and neighbor crowns the edifice of a fulfilled life, and makes a true love for oneself possible, a healthy self-esteem that shows us the measure in which we are to love others. Thus we come to see more clearly that the ambitious project of Christian maturity which is sanctity, means openness and concern for others, in order to help them share in our joy. "The Christian vocation by its very nature is also a vocation to the apostolate. No part of the structure of a living body is merely passive but has a share in

---

3. Francis, 269.

the functions as well as life of the body: so, too, in the body of Christ, which is the Church."[4]

If we look back from the top of our climb, everything falls into perspective. Faith, hope, and charity lead to a trusting abandonment, joined to the personal struggle to conform our life to Jesus as our model. We see engraved on our hearts the earth and the stars in the sky, our own being and God's law, so lovable and sure. We realize that the only true self-fulfillment possible, the only one that is worth the effort, is doing good facing God and our fellow men and women. And we launch out to fly.

We end these reflections on the characteristics of a mature Christian personality with the hope that they will be of help in confronting the challenge of becoming who we are. St. Josemaría's poetic words can serve as our conclusion:

"I see myself like a poor little bird, accustomed only to making short flights from tree to tree, or, at most, up to a third floor balcony. One day in its life it succeeded in reaching the roof of a modest building, that you could hardly call a skyscraper.

---

4. Vatican II, Decree *Apostolicam actuositatem*, 2.

"And lo and behold, our little bird is snatched up by an eagle, who mistakes the bird for one of its own brood. In its powerful talons the bird is borne higher and higher, above the mountains of the earth and the snowcapped peaks, above the white, blue and rosepink clouds, and higher and higher until it can look right into the sun. And then the eagle lets go of the little bird and says: Off you go. Fly!

"Lord, may I never flutter again close to the ground. May I always be enlightened by the rays of the divine sun—Christ—in the Eucharist. May my flight never be interrupted until I find repose in your Heart."[5]

Wenceslao Vial

---

5. Escrivá, *The Forge*, no. 39.

Works Cited

Augustine. *De fide rerum quae non videntur*, II.

———. *The City of God*, XIX.

Benedict XVI. Encyclical *Spe salvi*. November 30, 2007.

———. Homily on the Occasion of the Solemn Beginning of the Petrine Ministry of the Bishop of Rome. April 24, 2005.

———. Message for the 46th World Communications Day. May 20, 2012.

Dickens, Charles. "The Battle of Life." *The Christmas Books*, vol. 1. London: Penguin, 1972.

Escrivá, Josemaría. *Christ Is Passing By*. New York: Scepter Publishers, 2002.

———. *Conversations with Saint Josemaría*. New York: Scepter, 2007. Kindle Edition.

———. *Friends of God*. New York: Scepter, 1997.

———. *Furrow*. New York: Scepter, 1987.

———. "The Riches of the Faith." *ABC*. Madrid. (November 2, 1969)

———. Letter. February 2, 1945.

———. Letter. March 11, 1940.

———. *The Forge*. New York: Scepter, 1992.

———. *The Way*. New York: Scepter, 1992.

———. *The Way of the Cross*. New York: Scepter, 2011. Kindle edition.

Francis. Address before the Recital of the Holy Rosary. May 4, 2013.

———. Address on the Occasion of the Presentation of Letters of Credence. December 12, 2013.

———. Address to Participants in the Ecclesial Convention. June 17, 2013.

———. Address to Students and Teachers from the Seibu Gakuen Bunri Junior High School of Saitama, Tokyo. August 21, 2013.

———. Apostolic Exhortation *Amoris laetitia*. March 19, 2016.

———. Apostolic Exhortation *Evangelii gaudium*. November 24, 2013.

———. Encyclical *Laudato si'*. May 24, 2015.

———. General Audience. April 22, 2015.

———. General Audience. August 26, 2015.

———. General Audience. December 17, 2014.

———. General Audience. February 4, 2015.

———. General Audience. February 11, 2015.

———. General Audience. February 18, 2015.

———. General Audience, January 7, 2015.

———. General Audience. January 28, 2015.

———. General Audience. March 18, 2015.

———. General Audience. May 13, 2015.

———. General Audience. May 27, 2015.

———. Homily at Holy Mass for Families, Guayaquil. July 6, 2015.

———. Homily before the Image of Sancta Maria Salus Populi Romani. May 6, 2013.

———. Homily during the Pastoral Visit to Ancona. September 11, 2011.

———. Homily for the Family Day on the Occasion of the Year of Faith. October 27, 2013.

———. Morning Meditation in the Chapel of the Domus Sanctae Marthae. September 26, 2014. "True Identity," *L'Osservatore Romano*. Weekly ed. in English, n.40. October 3, 2014.

———. Morning Meditation in the Chapel of Domus Sanctae Marthae. October 10, 2014. In"The Heart on Guard," *L'Osservatore Romano*. Weekly ed. in English, n.42. October 17, 2014.

———. Prayer Vigil with the Young People during the Apostolic Journey to Rio de Janeiro for World Youth Day. July 27, 2013.

Frankl, Victor. *Man's Search for Meaning*. Translated by Ilse Lasch. Boston: Beacon Press, 2006.

John Paul II. Apostolic Exhortation *Familiaris consortio*. November 22, 1981.

———. Apostolic Letter *Rosarium Virginis Mariae.* October 16, 2002.

———. Encyclical *Redemptor hominis.* March 4, 1979.

———. Encyclical *Veritatis splendor.* August 6, 1993.

———. Letter to Artists. April 4, 1999.

———. Letter to Families. *Gratissimam sane.* February 2, 1994.

Letter to Diognetus, 5. (PG 2, 1174).

Medina, Javier. *Dora del Hoyo: A Lighted Lamp.* New York: Scepter, 2014.

Roman Missal, English Translation according to the Third Typical Edition. New York: Magnificat, 2011.

Teresa of Avila. *The Life of St. Teresa of Avila.* Translated by David Lewis. New York: Cosimo Classics, 2011.

Thérèse of Lisieux. "Offering to Merciful Love." June 9, 1895.

Thibon, Gustave. *Entre el amor y la muerte.* Madrid: Rialp, 1977.

Vázquez de Prada, Andrés. *The Founder of Opus Dei,* vol. I. New York: Scepter, 2001.

Vatican Council II. Decree *Apostolicam actuositatem.* November 18, 1965.

———. Pastoral Constitution on the Church in the Modern World—*Gaudium et spes.* December 7, 1965.

Recommended Reading

Burggraf, Jutta. *Made for Freedom: Loving, Defending and Living God's Gift.* New York: Scepter Publishers, 2012.

Cabanyes, Javier and Miguel Ángel Monge (eds.). *La Salud mental y sus cuidados.* Pamplona: Eunsa, 2011.

Covey, Stephen R. *The 7 Habits of Highly Effective People.* New York: Simon and Schuster, 2013.

Dweck, Carol S. *Mindset: The New Psychology of Success.* New York: Ballantine Books, 2007.

Esparza, Michel. *Self-Esteem Without Selfishness: Increasing Our Capacity for Love.* New York: Scepter Publishers, 2013.

Fernández-Carvajal, Francis. *Through Wind and Waves: On Being a Spiritual Guide.* New York: Scepter Publishers, 2012.

Frankl, Viktor. *Man's Search for Meaning.* New York: Beacon Press, 2006.

Harris, Russ and Steve Hayes. *The Happiness Trap: How to Stop Struggling and Start Living.* Boston: Trumpeter, 2008.

Kheriaty, Aaron and John Cihak. *The Catholic Guide to Depression.* Manchester, N.H.: Sophia Institute Press, 2012.

Lewis, Clive Staples. *The Four Loves.* New York: HarperCollins Publishers, 2017.

Martín, José M. (ed.). *Family Virtues: A Guide to Effective Parenting.* New York: Scepter Publishers, 2015.

Rojas, Enrique. *Love: The Great Opportunity.* Ediciones Planeta, Madrid: Ediciones Planeta, 2011.

Schlatter, Javier. *Wounds in the Heart: The Healing Power of Forgiveness.* New York: Scepter Publishers, 2015.

Sterner, Thomas M. *The Practicing Mind: Developing Focus and Discipline in Your Life.* Novato, CA: New World Library, 2005.

Vial, Wenceslao. *Madurez psicológica y espiritual.* Madrid: Palabra, 2016.

von Hildebrand, Dietrich. *The Heart: An Analysis of Human and Divine Affectivity.* Indiana: St. Augustine's Press, 2007.